Do IT Lean
Dave Collings

ISBN-13: 978-1522919162
Editor: Sonja Thompson
Cover Art: Sudabeh(Sudi) Farahmand

Table of Contents

4 The Foundation   58

5 Plan   68

6 Get Organized   77

15 Apps, Services, and Printers 154

16 Application Delivery 160

17 Special Projects 166

18 Management 173

Foreword

Dave and I have worked together for over 28 years. My background is in Accounting. We have had to deal with many short-term problems and create long-term solutions in a manufacturing environment.

Dave's experience in IT has simplified many headaches. We have utilized many of the topics that he is discussing in this book. Costing, labour reporting, work in process and month end reporting are all areas that have been addressed. From shop floor management to custom applications to standards and procedures and all areas in between, this book covers many of the traps that organizations fall into and offers solutions to avoid these problems. For anyone looking to start, improve or re-configure their business, this book is a must read.

The methods that Dave shares are tried and true. These pages are a valuable resource for organizations wanting a better understanding of their IT department and how they can improve business practices.

~ Denis Normandin

Introduction

This is a book primarily about SMB manufacturing and Lean IT. The use of IT in manufacturing is quite different from its use in other areas of business, like the finance industry. The manufacturing business needs to make some custom physical object or widget that meets the customers' requirements.

I have been working in small manufacturing businesses for over 30 years, performing various jobs or tasks from Design Engineer, CNC machine operator, NC programmer, to IT Manager. I would like to start out by providing some background information on myself and some of my experiences. This will lay a foundation for the remainder of the material. I hope you enjoy the journey.

Also, keep in mind that this is fairly high-level material to cover the broad range of things that are required to run an IT operation for a manufacturing Small Medium Business (SMB). Diving deep into any one of the topics within could very easily be another book by itself.

When we talk about lean IT, it's not a way to cheat software licensing or get around purchasing licenses. Instead, lean IT is about doing what's right for the business and keeping it cost effective. It involves people and process together with the right technology.

Getting Started

My purpose is to show some common sense approaches to the IT operation of a SMB. It's a good reference guide for anyone who needs to manage IT operations for an SMB, though more emphasis and examples are given to the business of manufacturing.

Specific mentions of hardware or software vendors are solely for the sake of reference. Software or hardware selection or preference is purely that of the SMB or unique situation of the business requirement.

I try not to go into a lot of specific details, because I assume that most people reading this are familiar with IT systems in general. My information and examples try to get to the heart of the issue and provide some clear, useful points.

This book has two major sections. The first 10 chapters, Part 1, cover the core fundamental pieces that I believe need to be in place to properly manage IT for a small business. The remainder of the chapters, Part 2, shows how to use and leverage that base of core fundamental pieces.

Chapter 1, Part 1

Definitions

Here are some acronym definitions that will help explain things as you read through the book. These are some not so common IT acronyms.

CAD/CAD- Computer aided Design/Computer aided Manufacturing, refers to computer software that is used to both design and manufacture products.

NC - Numerical Control, A program that controls a CNC machine.

CNC - Computerized Numerical Control, Computer control of machine tools.

2D - A 2 dimension drawing, a part print to manufacture an item.

3D - Three dimension, referred to as the CAD Database modelled in X,Y,X space.

RS232 and RS422 - A form of communication between a computer and machine. A standard for transmission of data.

ERP - Enterprise Resource Planning, Business process management software.

ISO - International Standards Organization, an international standard-setting body composed of representatives from various national standards organizations.

1 The beginning

Before we dive into lean IT, I'd like to give you, the reader, an understanding of where I came from and how my background and knowledge play a part in this book. Bear with me in this chapter while I lead you down a brief overview of my past.

College Days

In 1982, I started in the Mechanical Engineering Techniques program at Durham College. When I graduated, I was a fairly good machinist. I loved machining and being able to fabricate various things from metal. I got my first job offer at a small machine shop in Port Perry, but after careful consideration, I declined their offer. Being somewhat discouraged by the pay rate and work conditions, I returned to college and completed the Mechanical Engineering Technology program with the CAD/CAM option (Computer aided Design/Computer aided Manufacturing).

One of the best lessons I learned while attending college was how to think and apply what I knew or what I was taught to any given situation. I have always been very curious as to how things work and how to step up and find solutions when faced with problems. I was always looking for the next challenge or how to make things better.

After I graduated from the Technology program in 1985, I worked for a blow moulding company. The company had just purchased a new CAD/CAM system and their first Computer Numerical Control (CNC) machine. My job was to learn how to design blow moulds and CNC machine them from a solid block of aluminum. This was something new to the industry, and the company had started a research and development program to figure it out.

The Beginning of CAD/CAM

My graduating class were some of the first people in the manufacturing industry that came out of school and were fully trained in this new thing called CAD/CAM. Salaries were good and jobs were easy to come by, because a lot of manufacturers were anxious to get on board with these revolutionary new tools that few people knew how to use or implement.

This was pretty much the first time complete tooling designs were being performed in full 3D. Tooling was designed from three-dimensional CAD parts, and then it was fully CNC machined. Our process at the blow moulding company was nearly fully automated by our efforts. We created standards for tooling, developed feeds and speeds, fully automated hole drilling, and no 2D drawings were issued to the shop floor. For 1987, we were way ahead of our time in the manufacturing process of blow moulding design and manufacture.

Lack of Skill in CAD/CAM

It was an awesome opportunity to work in a small shop and be one of the first people to do something new. The CAD/CAM systems we worked on were called Computervision. There were no skilled IT people to install and configure these systems. It was up to us, the users, to install and configure new software when it came out. We were even responsible for day-to-day maintenance tasks like backups and user creation.

Back then, these systems had their own integrated programming languages, Newvar and Varpro. Even though end users had to perform the system automation and development, the tools were actually quite good and fairly easy to use. This helped us automate many of our processes.

Growth and Complexity

Moving on from plastics, I got into the die cast tooling business. I spent the majority of my career at a die cast tooling company. Coming from and R&D environment, I had a vast amount of experience. The tooling company had the same Computervision system, and defining standards and custom development was something they desperately needed.

Early on, I led a team to establish the part naming scheme and NC program naming and filing system. Reference is made to the team here, because the decision and naming standard was based on input and collaboration from the NC programming department. The company's current naming standards, at the time of this writing (20 plus years later), are still based on this same standard, even though it has evolved and been revised by various people and departments. This is an example of the importance of developing standards and how they improve over time.

Wearing Multiple Hats

While working as an NC programmer and CAD/CAM modeller, I also wore the hat of Systems Manager. As a Modeller, I was responsible for converting 2D-engineering drawings into 3D. This was the early days of CAD/CAM, when designing was still mostly done on the drafting table in 2D. The future was 3D, and everyone knew it. I was one of the people who had the 3D vision and ability to use a computer to convert the drawings to a CAD system. Once the conversion was complete, you could design the tooling in 3D.

After modelling and tool design, NC programs had to be created to cut the tooling. This was another task that I handled.

At the time, IT departments only existed in large companies. Small engineering firms had to figure it out themselves. I was naturally adapted for that role, because the language of computers and programming just came to me.

Eventually, I moved from design, NC programming over to IT. I had a huge advantage in IT supporting the business and users, because I came from the user side. I could relate to their headaches and frustrations. This assisted in getting down to the crux of problems and implementing solutions to resolve problems quickly.

Complete the Move to IT

When I made the move to IT, I had my work cut out for me. By this time, most small companies had IT departments, and I was mostly self-taught. So, I applied common sense and logic to establish a good base from where to start.

There were basically two sides of the business functioning but not really working together from an IT communication perspective. There were engineering and NC programming computers on their own network and business computers on their own network. There was no common network or data sharing between the two. BNC or coax media was commonly used for networks, because twisted pair was fairly new and expensive. The engineering side had high-end UNIX CAD workstations. The business side had Windows-based PCs with local storage. The storage infrastructure was in place for UNIX, so it was just a matter of installing one common network and getting the office computers accessing UNIX for storage and backup.

Along came a new network based on category 5 twisted pair (the best at the time). Samba was installed on UNIX to integrate Windows, UNIX storage, and share out printers. We then retrained all users on UNIX and Windows to save all their data on the network. Nothing was saved locally. Two network drives were released. The S:\ drive was for all users to store day-to-day work and share amongst each other. The P:\ drive was accessible by the individual user only. This was a secure place that users could store documents that only they were able to access—nobody else.

Of course, over time, things grew and became more sophisticated.

Chapter 2

2 About Manufacturing

What makes custom design and build manufacturing different compared to others types of businesses? With manufacturing, a custom physical object or widget needs to meet the customers' requirements. It has to be delivered on time and within the customers' specifications. This item must be designed, materials purchased, and components manufactured or subcontracted. The final product is then assembled, inspected, tested, and shipped to the customer.

Through the processes, CAD and PLM systems are used for the design, and ERP systems are used to purchase, receive, and help monitor and coordinate things through the shop floor. There's labor that goes into producing the item, including the machines' time that it takes to make the various components required for the end product. All these costs need to be captured and recorded for the specific job.

This is an over-simplification of the process, but I think it provides the general idea. Compare this to a pure financial corporation, where IT plays a much bigger role, because it is more critical to the functioning of the business, and there is seldom a need to produce a physical widget for a financial institution.

Another comparison is a new high-tech software company that's developing leading-edge solutions that rely heavily on IT, especially if the company is growing by hundreds of people each year. The demands on IT are massive and must be treated as such.

Yes, IT is still important to manufacturing, but it's not the core business. For manufacturers, the core business is making the widgets on time, within spec, and delivering them to the customer.

The Shop Floor

Manufacturing facilities have the majority of the building space set up to make their widgets. From an IT perspective, most of these machines have a PC-based controller and may run a Windows operating system, particularly on newer machines. The shop floor network ports are mapped and labeled just like the office. For distance purposes, the shop floor usually has centrally located wiring cabinets for network cables. These should all follow the same standard of labelling as the IT room so that everything is traceable. A good practice is to place log books in each wiring closet to track maintenance tasks.

In addition to centrally logged and managed documentation, I like to have a log book in each network cabinet. For technicians working on cabling issues, it's easy and practical to use this log book. It also helps the troubleshooting process, because you can quickly and easily see the most recent work done.

Machines

Within the shop floor, there are some machines that exist that help in the production process. These controllers also connect to the local network and receive machining information from network servers. In the case of the CNC machine, an application like PowerMILL is used to generate machine tool cutter location files (x, y, z moves). This data is commonly post-processed on the shop floor to specific code and sent to the machines. The data may be modified on the machines and then saved on network storage for future use. This is ideal if many identical jobs are repeated vs. one-off tasks.

On newer machines, the machine vendors expect remote access to the controls. Diagnostic tools exist within the controls that allow the vendor to check error logs or log directly onto the control and view it just like the local operator. I have seen custom client software or Virtual Network Computing (VNC) systems used for remote access.

It is not advisable to allow virtual private networks (VPNs) from the machine vendor to directly access your shop network, because the vendor has no idea what services are on your network or what they could inadvertently damage. Instead, let the vendor only remotely access the machines via a virtual desktop infrastructure (VDI), perhaps using a terminal services gateway. The VDI should only run the applications the vendor needs and connect to specified shop floor machines. It is also a good practice to control and manage access to the VDI computer so you know what the vendor is doing.

Since the controllers are PC-based, it's important to work with the maintenance department. IT may need to backup these machines and stock spare parts, system boards, or displays. Collaboration is crucial, since IT needs to know if new machines are coming in and what their function will be. Do they need network connection, remote access, or to be backed up? Get involved with other departments and listen to how IT can help improve the working conditions.

If the machines are very old, they may be using an RS232 or RS422 protocol and perhaps some very specific communication software. Serial communications are prone to their own quirks and errors. In the past, I have found it good practice to ground all CNC machines and use good quality shielded communications cables.

ERP

Within most manufacturing companies, an ERP system is in place that is used by all aspects of the business. In the ERP systems I am familiar with on the manufacturing side, a job gets defined. This job is considered what the customer ordered. The lot is a subset of the job and could contain a quantity. For example, under job 100, the customer orders three widgets of type A under lot 1 and two widgets of type B under lot 2. Cost reports allow the company to know what each individual widget, the sub component of a widget, or the entire job costs.

There are many ERP systems out there, and it is out of the scope of this book on how to select one for your business. However, I will mention some of the biggest challenges that ERP systems have with complex custom build manufacturing tooling environments:

• **Job costing.** Typically, this process is very complex in custom manufacturing tooling shops with standard off-the-shelf ERP systems, because it is very difficult to get all business divisions to stick to the processes and that all costs are properly attributed to the job/lot.

- **Scheduler limitations.** When dealing with large complex product structures, ERP scheduling engines can have problems. This is especially true when the production schedule is in a constant state of flux due to engineering changes or emergency repairs to production tooling. This flux creates a variance in flow with production.

- **Outside services.** This occurs when pieces in mid-process leave the building for some special treatment (heat treating, for example). It could even happen several times to the same piece throughout the manufacturing process.

- **Work in Progress (WIP) and job costing reports.** There are times when complex processes make it difficult to capture accurate costs. Large complex tooling can consist of thousands of parts and take several months to build, which poses a challenge for ERP systems.

To keep these issues to a minimum, it is important to put systems in place to catch processes when they start to fall off the rails. For job costing, you can restructure the General Ledger (GL) accounts so that all widget-making costs are associated with separate accounts. Then, it is possible for a given month to total the costs associated with making the widgets. Next, compare the total activity in the GL accounts for the same month. Theoretically, the totals should balance. If not, a series of reports could be generated to determine which items to make the widget are not having their costs captured correctly. This requires a close working relationship between IT, Purchasing, and Accounting. It also is extremely helpful to have people that understand and know the business working with IT. More than likely, there are rigid rules in place within the ERP system that need to be precisely followed so that costs will total correctly. This is the challenge within complex manufacturing processes.

Sometimes, it is required to justify the cost of hiring additional people to make sure the process is properly followed. This can be of value to improve the workflow of the business and capture the required data. With accurate data, strategic business decisions can be made. If a process continues to fail, than this means there's a problem that needs further investigation. Part of your processes in IT should be geared towards identifying problems and alerting the right people so that they can be solved.

Scheduling

Within the shop floor, there needs to be some method to schedule the activities, whether it's a scheduler that resides within the ERP system or a lean manufacturing pull system. I am not a master scheduler planner, but in discussions with lean consultants, I have leaned that some ERP schedulers have difficulty dealing with variable lead time and infinite capacity.

Variable lead time is the term used when the time to produce each piece is not consistent. This is commonly found in custom tooling manufacturing. Infinite capacity is a detailed scheduling strategy, when orders and operations are scheduled without considering the existing workload.

Planning the release of material in ERP systems on the shop floor might be appropriate for tooling shops, because the duration of the jobs are longer—several weeks or months vs. just in time (JIT) operations. JIT refers to a company whose function is to produce parts and ship them directly to a factory for assembly. This is ideal for a lean manufacturing pull system.

You can also choose to schedule manually and use the ERP system to track the location of all the widgets that compose the job. Imagine being able to ask the status of a job and have the system tell you exactly where all the components are located and their state of completion. This is possible with the Internet of Things (IoT) and a good ERP system. I will discuss this in more detail when talking about the future of SMB IT in Chapter 20.

For more information regarding lean manufacturing, I recommend Lonnie Wilson's book, *How To Implement Lean Manufacturing*.

Custom Applications

What can really set a part and improve a manufacturing operation? Customized applications will give a company a clear boost over their competitors. However, this can very easily become a double-edge sword. Customization can help you, but it can also lock your business into a specific software or revision of the software. Put some serious thought behind the decision before customizing applications.

It is also possible to submit custom enhancements to software vendors so that they maintain the releases and updates. I have worked with ERP vendors and NC software vendors for these enhancements in the past. Make sure you understand the impact to your business and have a plan for how to deal with supporting customizations moving forward.

I have an example from many years ago, when the company I worked for decided to make the ISO quality forms electronic and integrate them with workflow. At the time, nothing existed on the market that would meet the level of functionality required. The end results of this project were very successful. Not only did it enhance the flow of the forms, but a large amount of data was available for reporting and making further improvements. An additional benefit came when auditing the ISO 9000 system. The auditors loved the level of detail and audit trails built into the system.

The lesson here is to do your homework and make sure you really want to or need to create custom software.

Learn how to capture information and make more informed decisions by reading *The Rational Manager*, by Kepner and Tregoe.

Business Processes

Most manufacturing institutions that I'm familiar with have their own set of processes. Don't assume one manufacturing business works just like another, because each is typically unique to the type of work being done. If the business is to stamp out fenders for cars and trucks, it's a very different process for manufacturing the tooling that is used to stamp out the parts. Similar IT systems or software may be used in a financial or sales organization, but how they are used and implemented in manufacturing are very different.

Custom large tooling manufacturing often deals with a large install base of multiple complex applications. Many of the applications don't necessarily install well with competitors' products on the same physical desktop.

Let me give you an example. There are multiple CAD systems, including Siemens UG NX, CATIA, and SolidWorks. There are also multiple CAM software, such as PowerMILL, CATIA, Lemoine RTM, and Vericut. All of the software requires license servers that don't necessarily work together. In some cases, all of this software has to be installed on the same computer.

This is where my background in manufacturing is helpful, because I understand all of the business requirements and processes that make the task of juggling these requirements much easier.

Try to virtualize as many software licenses as possible onto as few license servers as possible. Don't waste time trying to get all the licenses to run on one server. It is common for vendors to release new licenses and license servers that require updating. Simply add more license servers. Some license servers require dedicated server hardware with license dongles, but don't install this on an Active Directory server. Get an older server, install an operating system compatible with the license software, and run that. Keep spare hard drives, power supplies, and fans around to support the server. A license server always needs updating and new licenses installed on a regular basis. So, keep it simple, and don't make your life difficult.

VDI may be a good solution for handling multiple CAD applications, like if you have customers that use different releases of UG NX and different versions of PLM. It is possible to build multiple VDI desktops for each customer. The engineer would launch a particular VDI workstation, depending on the customer or design he/she is working on.

IT's Primary Role is Service Manufacturing

Manufacturing is different than a financial institute or a marketing company. These latter companies value IT a bit more, because it is critical to the functioning of the business. In manufacturing, it is more critical to make widgets. When the machinery is down, that means no parts are made, which equates to no money.

IT is important as a supporting role to the manufacturing process. Any IT function that serves shop floor manufacturing directly is most critical, because machines can't run without it. Network, data storage, and shop floor PCs are a higher priority than a mail server or Internet connection, for example. An office workstation would take a lower priority than a workstation on the shop floor, because that one shop floor machine not working could result in a backlog of parts. You can do the math for your own environment as to the impact to the business.

A financial institution is much more sensitive to any of its IT systems being down and require a higher level of redundancy in their systems to compensate for outages. However, certain IT systems can be down for a short period of time without negatively impacting the company.

It's essential that you gather information about your business. Make a list of all the various departments, and then meet with the head of each department so that you can understand their processes. If it is a manufacturing business, don't treat the shop floor as one big department, because it is comprised of multiple departments or cells. Find out what each department does and their reliance on IT. Does an organizational chart exist for the company? If the company is ISO certified, they must have one. This is a good place to begin.

On your list of departments, include their concerns and any business issues. Add a column for things you can do that might help each department. For example, if they require data, perhaps you can generate a report from the ERP system. Once you have a list, reorganize it by priority. Which departments do you think, based on your research, impact the business process the most if they are down?

You can then use this information to generate checklists, polices, and procedures, which we will cover in more detail in subsequent chapters.

Chapter 3

3 Keep IT Simple

This is the most challenging part of the job, and experience really helps. If you are new to manufacturing, there will be people lining up at the door to get what they want. Listen to their concerns, make notes, plan, and prioritize.

Don't Complicate

There are many ways to keep your systems simple. However, you must first make sure that there won't be a negative impact on the business. It is essential that you have the support of upper management and that they know why things are done the way they are. For example, end users shouldn't install hardware or software unless it's absolutely necessary. You're not enforcing this because you're a grumpy IT person and want control over everything. Instead, you're responsible for the overall running of the systems that support the business day to day. A balance must be struck between giving users what they need and being able to service all IT operations within the business at a reasonable cost.

There will be people within the organization that think they are the center of the universe and expect to get everything they want. Remember, it is your job to service the entire company, not just one person, and there's an operating budget that you need to stick to. These people that expect everything need to know that a budget exists, and there are reasonable limitations. It is your job to report issues and challenges to the management team so that a plan of action can be formulated that supports the needs of the business moving forward.

> *"The needs of the many outweigh the needs of the few."*
>
> *~ Spock, Star Trek II: The Wrath of Khan, 1982*

No Unnecessary Software

As in most environments, users tend to request and use any software they want. They don't care that it costs money. Some users even go out of their way to find free or shareware software. Take some time to assess the needs of the business, by department, and come to an agreement about what common software to use. There is no need to have four or five different picture-editing software, for example. Some cases may require more than one, but when you determine that, you can plan for it.

A good example is using Outlook instead of Exchange Outlook Web Access (OWA), which is basically a stripped-down version of Outlook. Here's the thing... if there's one less software to install, that's one less application to patch, update, and fix when updates break it (which happens). Also, Outlook is more sensitive to viruses or malware. So, keep it simple, and keep it lean. Discuss this with department heads to get their buy in and understanding. Typically, that's not a problem, because most people use web mail, like Gmail, for personal email.

If you read the book, *The Rational Manager*, by Kepner and Tregoe, there are some good charts for helping make decisions. Use them in this case and review your findings with department heads so that they are aware of the issues of using full Outlook vs. OWA. A cost analysis could also be done to show the increased effort to use Outlook over OWA. This is a small but valid example. At the end of the day, common sense must prevail.

When Common Sense isn't so Common

Almost everybody loves new technology and what it can do. I do, and I'm a bit of a gadget freak as well. I love searching for a new app for my phone that will do exactly what I want and browsing the latest mobile OS release so I can explore the newest enhancements.

However, the "latest and greatest" isn't always necessary.

For example, Office 365 is a truly awesome product. Let's say that you have a manufacturing facility with an existing install of Office 2013 that is paid for and there are no subscriptions. Office 365 comes with full remote desktop support for mobile users with laptops, tablets, and smartphones, but this functionality would only benefit 10-12% of your users. Does it make business sense to purchase Office 365 now or wait until you need to update the existing Office 2013 install? You can do the math for your own business to see if the cost is justifiable and if the benefits truly enhance the operation of the business.

If there's already a process in place to deal with much of what Office 365 has to offer today, consider waiting to upgrade to Office 365 until a business need requires you to do so. Analyze the rest of the business to see if it makes more sense to put the funds somewhere else. Perhaps the storage server is five plus years old, getting too slow, and should be replaced instead. I believe that money should be spent on what the business needs today instead of new, whiz-bang technology that has little current benefit to the business.

Don't Allow Users to Install Software

To keep things under control and resources manageable in Active Directory, set up general users so that they can't install software. This is your first simple line of defense if some virus or malware gets released on your network. If the user can't install software, this reduces the chance a virus can spread. Also, keep everyone in line with the directive to use common software instead of allowing them to use whatever software they like. This is very important in a manufacturing environment where standards need to be created and followed.

Again, management support is critical here. You need the support of senior management so that you have the authority and responsibility to deliver. Don't confuse this with IT bullying. Instead, this is business common sense. At the end of the day, common sense must prevail.

> *"Leadership is about common sense, which unfortunately, is not all that common."*
> *~ Robert Lutz, Guts: 8 Laws of Business from One of the Innovative Business Leaders of Our Time*

Some organizations allow users to freely install any software they think will help them be productive. In a manufacturing environment, this can very quickly work against you. For example, it's common in an NC programming environment that users are able to fluently share projects. NC programming typically works two shifts: day and night. If problems arise on night shift and someone on day shift made the program, it doesn't make sense for the machine on the shop floor to sit idle all night.

The NC programming is performed in a 3D CAM system, such as PowerMILL. With PowerMILL, the users all discuss and decide naming and filing standards, Colour standards, tool name standards, plus NC program and file names. They also decide, as a group, all the other software used for doing setup sheets, tool path verification, and any standard functions within the software. The entire process can become quite complex. So, the value of agreeing on what software to use and how to use it is important. If there's not an agreement, it's impossible for other people to open the file and work with the data.

When it comes to lean concepts, agree on the standard, teach the standard, and make it visible.

I will make one final statement here and a slight retraction. For very small businesses, say around 10 people, not as many controls will be required. A small, close group of people can easily function like a family, where they know and understand their contribution to the business. They know that if they surf the Internet to unsafe places or install some unknown software, there could be negative effects that could harm their performance. In these types of cases, the business will be more self-regulating. In order to do the right thing for the business, get to understand the business and how it functions.

Standards, Policies, and Procedures

Standards, policies, and procedures are helpful to get new staff up to speed, establish standard methods to perform tasks, and implement safeguards based on lessons that were learned.

Standards get people to collaborate and share data, because it takes a group effort to define the standard, and doing so increases productivity. Every time someone goes to do a task, a standard can be followed. A standard also provides a baseline from which staff can be measured against.

I start with standard document templates for documenting install processes. These documents are then stored in a predefined hierarchy. The template and hierarchy is discussed and decided by people within the IT department. Everyone's thoughts and ideas are incorporated into how the filing system works. This is ideal for motivating and making people feel as though they are part of the team.

When creating polices, start with simple things like "Don't install new applications to production server or desktops without testing and gathering feedback." Another policy is "Never install on a Friday, when production runs on the weekend and at night." You don't want a disaster to interrupt production over a weekend and loose valuable time. It is better to ease the install in during the early part of the week so that things can be monitored more closely and repaired quickly. Plan before doing. If you're performing an installation or update, think about the process first, write the steps down, make a checklist, and then follow it. More than likely, if a checklist or plan is not made, you'll come across something unexpected and have to delay the task until the problem or issue has been resolved.

Another policy is for "General network and Internet use." This should be provided to all employees at the time of hiring, signed, and saved for reference. It describes the types of conduct that you allow within the corporate network. There are several examples of what constitutes as acceptable and unacceptable Internet use, and it should be created to suite the needs of your business.

For business procedures, first plan, then use the standard document templates and have a ticketing system to report and track all problems. It's extremely important to keep a history of what has taken place, so if the problem comes back, you know how to fix it —or if something goes wrong, you know how to undo it and continue on. Create a backup before making a change, even if it's something as simple as updating a smartphone for a user. This is especially true for older devices. If the update fails, the backup can be restored and return the device to its original state.

Here is a good example. I gave one of my junior staff a small project. Their simple task was to synchronize all the files from system A to system B. The servers were across a very slow WAN, so copies had to be kept on both systems. My staff member tested several options, and when I asked for a summary, he said the option that he selected was fast and did all of these wonderful things. When I asked how it compared to the other synchronization options, he replied that he couldn't remember exactly, but the one he chose was the best. However, there needed to be a list of requirements. The primary goal was speed throttling, since we had to be able to throttle the speed way down, so the fastest option wasn't helpful. It was already determined that Distributed File System (DFS) would not work in this case. So, the staff member had to go back to the drawing board and start with a plan, list out what needed to be tested, and define the criteria.

In the book *The Rational Manager,* references are made for a matrix that can be used to aid in the decision-making process. It may not be required for simple scenarios, but it is well worth the effort when making bigger decisions.

I highly recommend that you implement the following procedures:

1. **User Creation.** What department do users belong to? What role do they have? Which applications do they need to access?

2. **User Removal.** What is the correct process to remove a user?

3. **Patches.** What is the procedure to push out Windows patches?

4. **Backup.** What is the proper backup procedure?

Documentation

Creating proper documentation is critical for managing day-to-day operations. You don't need some fancy high-priced software to manage your documents. Just use a system that works for your business requirements. It's ultimately up to the people doing the documentation to understand why they need to document, how to save it, and in what format.

For a small manufacturing business, a good folder structure with logical names is a solid place to start. Any key server for the business should have a process documented so that it can be recreated from the beginning (bare metal install), which is useful for disaster recover installs. I also highly recommend having server backup images for every server. This provides a safe recover point in case of a disaster.

Through the life of the server, every configuration or change needs to be tracked. Why? If a change is made and problems arise, you'll know exactly what has been changed so that it's easy to undo or troubleshoot. This may be one of the easiest ways to fix a problem.

Changes and problems should also be documented in a change management system. Again, you don't need high-priced, fancy software. Keep it simple! Pick a system that will do the job and grow with the business.

Status Meetings (Transparency)

One of my standards is to have weekly proactive status meetings, typically held early Monday mornings, just after everyone gets to work and settles in. These are primarily operational meetings. The purpose is to have everyone on the same page with regard to tasks that are under way and review any major problems.

This is also an ideal time to get to know your people better and understand them and issues that they are struggling with. Allocate some time to discuss the bigger picture, like how IT is actively helping the business overall. Discuss big projects on the go, like how the ERP is enhancing new reporting services and automating report delivery to people when they want it. This will help your staff understand the positive effects of their work on the business.

I don't believe in hiding information from people. If one of your staff is working on a project, they need to understand the bigger picture and gather information from as many people as possible, including end users who may have experienced problems. Allowing people to do research on their projects is a challenge, and it gives them a sense of responsibility.

Get to know the people within your business and department. Learn to communicate with each one of them in a way that works. Every person is different. Understand this and make it work for you. People work differently, so don't force them to conform to a strict set of rules, and don't micromanage.

Managing

Here is my philosophy on managing people. When you have standards, policies, and procedures in place, teach them to your staff, and make them visible. Everyone should be involved in the process of defining them, and they can be modified, changed, or updated as needed. You can measure how well your people perform based on the defined standards, policies, and procedures. By raising the standard, people work towards improving the entire process.

Provide regular feedback so that people know how they're doing. A good manager will be able to touch on the problem points where an employee needs to improve without leaving a negative feeling. The key is to make sure your people are in a positive state and motivated to move forward.

It's also important to set goals—both personal goals and department goals. For example, one of our goals was concerning the maximum time a production desktop computer could be down. We determined that was one hour from the time the IT department heard about it to the completion of the fix. One person was responsible for this operation—to come up with a plan, implement it, and achieve the goal. He or she could modify or change the process as needed to meet the requirement. Since keeping production running is extremely important to the business, these goals are often discussed as a group during the regular status meetings.

In Lonnie's book about lean manufacturing, he says, "Tell me how a man is measured and I will tell you how he will behave." This is a very true statement, and it needs to be absolutely clear in everyone's mind what their job is and how they will be measured doing it.

Micromanagement is counterproductive, because it stops people from thinking and removes any sense of responsibility and authority. People need to feel like they belong. They need the responsibility and authority to do their jobs. Processes and procedures can't run by themselves, so people are required to execute them. Ultimately, people are the key to any successful operation.

You should also manage people differently, depending on their personality type. One example is introverts vs. extroverts. What are they and how does this impact management? An extrovert is a person who gains energy from other people. They recharge by being social, and they're typically loud spoken and like to control the conversation. Introverts, on the other hand, recharge when they're alone and loose energy in crowds. They crave peace and quiet but aren't necessarily shy.

One of the biggest trends I've seen in North America is that extroverts control many management positions. I find that most managers as extroverts lack the ability to make sure everyone is involved or equally heard. However, everyone needs to have some level of involvement in the process. A manager or leader must be aware of this.

Extroverts tend to speak out loud and often out of turn to get what they want, because they think their opinion is the most important. Introverts may not speak in a meeting, but they'll go away, absorb the information, and come back to the table with some out-of-the-box thinking. Visit this website to more clearly understand introverts and their abilities: http://www.quietrev.com.

There are a lot of resources where you can learn more about different personality types. Read the articles that make sense to you, and only use the parts you feel are appropriate. The book, "*Do What You Are: Discover the Perfect Career for You Through the Secrets of Personality Type*," by Paul D. Tieger and Barbara Barron-Tieger, will help you determine your personality type, and it can also help you to find a fitting career.

As a manager, you should know how to adjust and adapt to working with different types of people. Do what is right for you, your people, and your business. Above all, keep it simple.

Terminal Servers

Terminal servers are extremely useful. I've used them to host desktops where many users perform light duties and use the same applications or use a client application like ERP. Instead of installing the client application on every desktop, put it in one place and have the users remotely connect to the terminal server to host the application. I call this process layering.

Build the foundation solid with a network that is fast. Size the network for more than is required today. Build it to be expandable, and create the core to be faster by at least three or four times. If this is done right, it will last five to eight years or longer, so build in redundancy.

Servers should be similar, so use faster processors and more memory than required. This will give the server more usable life. Planning is important. If you work in manufacturing, remember that the primary goal of the business is to produce widgets.

Once the core is strong, layer in the required applications on terminal servers. Place all commonly used day-to-day applications on the primary terminal server. This is the server that all users log into for their main desktop. When launching applications like ERP, the session should run on its own dedicated server. The same thing can be done with specialty applications for accounting, like ADP.

This makes it easier to upgrade to new systems. The core server is left as-is, then a new terminal server with upgraded applications can be built and seamlessly slid into production with no impact to the users.

Another benefit of terminal servers is if one of your applications moves to the cloud, it can be layered in the same way. This is planning for the future with built-in flexibility.

Desktop Images

Wherever possible, make your life simple. If desktops or laptops are used for power users, have them all based from a standard Windows install image. Reduce the need to install what I call one-off applications. There are times these will be required, but try to layer them in using terminal services. This reduces the total number of unique desktop images and enables faster deployment.

In an engineering environment, there are several oddball applications that don't allow for easy central or automated install methods. Windows does have an AIK toolkit to automate the installs of Windows desktops. From past experience, it requires significant effort to setup and maintain these tools, but it's well worth it if you have a large business, the need, and resources to support it.

For smaller manufacturing businesses, I recommend using standard Microsoft Windows backup tools to create and deploy base images. You should also create custom scripts using Windows Sysinternals PsTools to automate application installs and updates. Sysinternal PsTools is easy to learn, and you can run the reusable scripts after the base images have been pushed to computers.

The other tool I like from Microsoft is System Center Endpoint Protection. This has become a very powerful tool for detecting viruses and malware and pushing out Windows updates. It's a one-stop shop for securing desktops. I preferred the user interface of the older version, called Forefront Endpoint Protection, but it's still a solid product and does the job well.

Depending on the size and demands of your business, you may want to investigate and use more of the functionality within System Center Essentials. However, the more functionality you use, the more complexity deepens. My philosophy is to keep it simple and don't add complication where it's not required.

Standard Hardware

Find a hardware vendor you like for desktops, storage, network, and servers. It's very important to keep your hardware the same as much as possible. This makes image deployment faster and easier.

Instead of purchasing support contracts for desktops, I prefer keeping spare parts and extra desktops on hand. A side benefit of having extra desktops is that you can set up a training lab to test new software and install updates. Replacement parts are typically easy to purchase if you use brand name hardware, like HP. The replacement cycle for a high-end workstation is three years on average. After that, they start to become too slow. It's best to purchase hardware in bulk, with identical quantities so that less spare parts are required, and they can be interchangeable.

For example, with the purchase of 20 new computers, add two power supplies, a disk, and memory. If a computer doesn't fail within the first year, it will likely last three years. In the second and third years, the odd power supply, memory, and disk will fail. Doing this is less expensive than a support contract in the long run. However, be sure to work the math for your own business case and hardware.

Another advantage of having spare hardware is that the turnaround to get a computer back online is much faster. Remember, in a production environment, if a PC is connected to a machine, every hour the machine is down costs money—not just the hourly rate of that machine, but also the backlog of work that gets created.

Apply the same logic to servers. Always keep a spare disk, memory, and power supplies on hand. These days, almost everyone uses virtual computing. If you have 12 or 15 computers on one physical server, it's a good idea to have spare parts and a service contract. More than likely, a hardware failure on the hypervisor server is critical. So, be prepared and plan for what could happen. Try to purchase identical hypervisor servers when many are required.

Even if your equipment is under warranty or you have a service contract, keep some spare parts handy. Some manufacturing facilities may be physically located in areas that don't have same-day delivery service. Take this into account when purchasing new hardware. Also, keep in mind that manufacturing firms tend to keep hardware longer—and the older the hardware, the more difficult it is to find spare parts. This is a good reason to buy quality, brand name hardware, where parts are more plentiful.

At some point in the future, I believe VDI will fully replace standard desktop hardware. In some small cases today, manufacturing SMBs can justify the cost between desktops and VDI. The technology is maturing, and the cost is coming down to a point where it's more affordable. You can easily perform a cost calculation for your business. However, you should first check all the applications in use within your organization to make sure they fully support VDI. Within an engineering environment, it's fairly common to find several odd-ball application that have issues. Eventually, all applications will support VDI.

VDI has been around for many years. Back in the late 1990s, all high-end CAD systems were UNIX-based. PCs were way cheaper, so we had to think of ways to bring down the cost of the system or increase productivity. Our solution was to create low-cost PC-based terminal servers to run an application called Vericut. NC programming was performed on UNIX workstations, because it was the only architecture that it could run on, but the verification software ran on Windows PCs. It was very cost effective to host up to eight verification sessions on a server and certainly less expensive than purchasing and maintaining eight PCs.

Citrix was used for the terminal server and connected to UNIX using ICA Client software, which was the best at the time for 3D-graphics performance. Vericut used to be installed on the UNIX workstation, but it was cheaper to license on a PC and ran faster, because the process and load was split across two platforms—NC programming on UNIX and Vericut on a PC. This isn't required today, because PCs have so many cores that both applications can run on the same computer without affecting one another. CAD Engineering design workstations are a better fit for VDI, because they don't demand as much CPU power. NC programming, verification, and structural analysis applications are extremely CPU and memory intensive and perform better on dedicated hardware for an SMB.

VDI basically hosts a virtual desktop PC for each user in the data center, with equal graphic performance. The big advantage here for engineers is they can easily access their full desktop anywhere and from any device, as long as they have an Internet connection. VDI also nicely flows into the cloud. At some point in the future, it's quite possible that this may be the only way to access licensed applications.

Best of Breed Software

I've heard many salesmen make the statement, "Oh, I really prefer best of breed software." What does that really mean? It can largely be associated with "very expensive." There are times when you need the very best software available to do your job, but not always. Software should accomplish the job that you need to complete—nothing more, and nothing less.

Another pitch you may hear when evaluating software is, "We have a special for the end of the month, if you buy now." This could be true, but if your plan is to evaluate three types of software for a particular task, stick to the plan and don't get sidetracked by a sales tactic.

Make sure that you think carefully about your environment and what you need. Don't overdo things and pay additional money for services. There's often no need to add complex management software that takes resources to maintain and can incur additional licensing costs. Plan for the future and business growth. Size your servers and desktops to last for three to five years, with additional RAM and computing power. However, it's equally important not to underestimate your needs. Servers should always have mirrored hard drives and redundant power supplies. I actually make this a standard.

When storing your spare parts, apply the lean methodology: keep it simple, and make it visible. I typically write on the box what the parts are for and then place it on a shelf where it's visible. Allocate some shelf space for these things. You can keep the shelves narrow and high so that it doesn't consume much space. Honestly, it's only a matter of time before a mechanical hard drive and power supplies fail, so it makes good business sense to have spare parts to keep the servers running in top performance.

Chapter 4

4 The Foundation

Many small organizations may or may not have a data center. Perhaps they simply call it an IT room. Nonetheless, the same basic principals apply. I'm not going into great detail here, because there are plenty of other resources that can provide guidance on how to construct a proper place to house critical servers. However, there are certain basic core requirements for managing your infrastructure.

I call these requirements the foundation, because it is like the foundation of your house. If you build it right, it will last a long time and be easy to maintain. If you build it poorly, it will collapse, or all your time will be spent maintaining and fixing foundation problems.

Firmware, Windows Updates, Malware, and Viruses

These are basic services and/or functions that small businesses need to plan for and manage. All hardware has firmware for various things—ILO if it's HP, DRAC if it's Dell, etc. When a new server is built and released, it's important to make sure all firmware is up to date. Once the server has been released to production and is running stable, I don't update the firmware unless there's a problem that a firmware update will solve. I have seen damage and systems fail by trying to stay on top of firmware updates to production servers. Keep ILO devices on internal networks whenever possible. If they aren't exposed to the Internet, you shouldn't have to worry about critical security fixes. Don't add to your workload. Remember to keep it simple.

If older hardware is being reused and deployed on a newer operating system, do your homework, plan, prepare, and update firmware if required. Make sure all the hardware devices are fully supported on the new operating system. When it comes to key servers, leave nothing to chance. Do it right. Glance through the release notes for your hardware and keep them handy in case problems arise.

To keep your environment secure, you must perform Windows critical fixes and security updates. A good practice is to have several production desktops and servers that aren't critical to business allocated in a test group, and keep them current with the latest updates. This will provide some level of confidence that the updates won't break things that are running in your environment. Keep all other desktops and servers at least one month behind. This way, if there are issues with updates, they can be fixed by Microsoft before the rest of your computers are updated.

Again, keep it simple and don't make extra work for yourself. Chasing down and fixing problems incurred by Windows updates is no small task. It could take hours, days, and even weeks to solve some problems. Some release notes for updates include details about what they will fix or break. Some updates change the default security setting in IE, which can easily break older applications that have been running flawlessly. The message here is to not blindly update all your Windows desktops and servers to the latest patch levels without first testing them.

To keep systems up to date and patched, plus malware and viruses under control, you should have a good management tool, like Microsoft's System Center Essentials with Endpoint Protection. Windows Server Update Services (WSUS) is a free add-on that pushes out patches and updates. Endpoint Protection manages virus, scans for malware, and updates the definition files. This Windows product fits nicely within the Windows management framework.

Climate and Air Flow

In any IT room, it's very important to have adequate cooling. Cool air comes in at the front of the computers and exits out the back. Make sure equipment is mounted correctly in the racks so that air flows in the front and out the back. Don't mount some devices in backward, which goes against the flow of air.

Place air conditioning diffusers at the front of your servers. Plan for a dual A/C unit, because one can fail. Make sure your A/C units are on a service contract so that they are maintained on a regular basis. If the IT room is small and has a fair number of servers, it can be difficult to keep the temperature constant. For small rooms where air flows into the front of the servers, shoot for 20 to 21 degrees Celsius —and where the air exits, it will be 25 or 26 degrees Celsius, or even warmer right near the servers.

Humidity is not as critical these days, but 40-55% relative humidity is sufficient. Too much humidity will cause corrosion, and too little humidity will promote static electricity. It's also a good practice to have temperature and humidity sensors in the room that monitor the environment and let you know if things start to get out of hand.

Lastly, make sure all server cabinets and telecom racks are grounded. This will keep them stable and protect them from static electricity.

Physical Security

It's very important to restrict access to your most critical servers at all times. You don't want to have strangers or janitors roaming around your server room. Unskilled people in your IT room can easily damage or turn off equipment without even knowing it. Keep your IT room locked. Only allow people who require access to enter the IT room. Keep a sign-in sheet if the room is in a remote office with no IT people present. It's good to know who goes in and out of the room and what they were doing. This information can be useful for troubleshooting problems.

Many years ago, I learned the importance of physical security. We used to allow cleaning staff into our IT room. This wasn't a problem until one of our servers started shutting down at night. Upon closer inspection, the cleaning staff decided that it was easier to plug his vacuum into an outlet in the IT room. He would simply unplug the server to vacuum, and then plug it back in again when he was done. This lesson certainly reinforced the need for constant physical security.

Visual

The IT room should be visually appealing and organized. Keep everything stored in its proper place when it's not in use. Colour-code your cabling, and then label and document what the cables are for. This includes labeling each end of your power cables so that they can be traced to the PDU or UPS. Identify servers on the front and back of the devices. Labeling must be clear, neat, and concise. Be sure to include any documentation that goes with the server—network switches, tape drives, consoles, and external drives. Server cabinets and communication racks all need to be identified and labeled as well.

Elevation diagrams depict server U-heights. Network port maps indicate which ports plug into which servers or devices. All these tools are essential for troubleshooting problems. It makes it very easy to identify everything that belongs to a device so that it can be traced.

Power

All server and network switches should have clean power and be connected to some sort of a UPS. The core IT room must have a backup generator. Over the last several years, I've noticed a definite change of weather patterns in Ontario, Canada. There have been many major storms where the municipal power goes down for several days. So, keeping clean, stable power to the IT room is essential. Even for a small business, the power going off for extended periods of time can be problematic, especially for older equipment, which may have difficulty coming back online. Basically, electronic equipment that has been up and running for a long period of time is more stable. Whenever possible, avoid turning the power off to devices, power supplies, and disk drives.

Again, this is where spare parts come in handy. Even with all the safeguards in place, you can still experience power failure. If your IT room is located in your manufacturing facility, it's most likely not the caliber of a Tier 3 data center. Make sure the power comes from a circuit that's isolated from manufacturing equipment, and draw the power from an isolated transformer.

Backup generators are also important, but they need constant maintenance so that they continue to run when required. Install remote software for your generator and configure it to alert you if there's a problem.

Cabling

Colour-code the cabling for each department, server, room, or floor. Organize it however you want. This is great for troubleshooting, because it makes it easier and faster to locate problematic cables.

All cabling should have a label on each end that follows the naming standard that you've established. When you look at the end of a cable that is correctly labelled, there should be no confusion as to where to plug it in.

Around the back of the servers, make sure the cabling is securely fastened with Velcro to the sides of the server cabinet. No cables should be blocking the airflow on the back of the server.

When you step back and look at the cabling, there shouldn't be any loose unlabelled patch cables in use. If there are, consider it a temporary patch, and assign it a specific Colour. Any time this Colour cable is seen, it indicates a) it's temporary and/or b) it's for test purposes.

For structured and patch cabling, I use the most current cable available, which is category 6 at the time of this writing. Solid cabling is ideal for structured runs, so that your cables don't move. Stranded cables are better for patch runs, because they are moved and bent more frequently. Use the highest quality cabling that's available, because you'll typically get more life out of it, and you really don't want to have to mess around with cabling issues.

Back when category 4 was commonly used, category 5E was available. For all new cabling runs, I bought category 5E. Today, I'm still able to use the same cabling, and I safely run a full 1 GB over it.

Having said this, you should ultimately do what is right for your business. Calculate the cost of the cabling, plan for the future, and do what makes the most sense.

Network Switches

Is it really necessary to have the "best of breed" switches for smaller businesses? Are layer 3 switches really required? Honestly, if there's no need for complexity, don't do it. This is the "keep it simple" philosophy.

Cisco probably makes one of the best and most reliable switches available. Use them for extremely important operations where uptime and stability are critical. However, D-link switches for example, can be purchased for a fraction of the price, and they're sufficient for most SMB needs.

Check point also makes quality firewalls, but both Barracuda and Pfsense have suitable firewall products at reasonable prices. Barracuda's firewall has an easy-to-use graphical interface that's good for SMBs, where many IT people wear multiple hats and perform numerous jobs. The Pfsense firewall also has a nice graphical interface, but it's more flexibly and a bit more complex than Barracuda.

Again, do your homework, plan, and figure out what is right for your business.

Contacts and Password Lists

Why do you want to keep a list of contact and passwords? Simple. When problems arise, and you need to contact your ISP, you don't want to waste time looking for the details of your contract. You should be able to open a document and get the contact support number and other information you need. The same thing goes for password lists, because no one can remember them all. Keep the lists in secure locations, and make sure the documents are password protected.

Chapter 5

5 Plan

Planning is the most frequently missed step in most SMB IT processes. I have observed so many people jump in feet first and struggle to fix a simple problem. However, it would be much easier to take a step back, look at what has to be done, write it out, and then proceed.

Project Plan

Good project plans are required for large-scale projects that involve many resources over a long period of time, and where the project has the girth for a full-time project planner. However, the majority of projects on the go in a small manufacturing business only require a task list. Apply common sense, and do what is right for your business.

Project planning is a complete book all by itself, but I would like to point out the importance and the need when required.

Task List

The day-to-day running of an operation requires the use of task lists. This allows IT resources to assign daily tasks that are typically fairly short in duration. A small team of people can easily manage task lists by creating and sharing a Google Sheet. Each person on the team has their own dedicated tab. Break each Sheet into multiple columns: number, description, due date, and status. Divide each sheet into sections for simple tasks or longer projects. This is an easy way for everyone to know what's going on. Have the IT team keep this Sheet open on their desktop for quick access and updates. These can be reviewed at weekly meetings or one-on-one meetings as required. You can also use them for tracking progress and goals.

Here's a good example of planning before doing. Some non-critical services had to be moved into a hosted environment. The client required remote access to the services from their local office. The current server was up and running in their local environment. The task was simple and should have been completed within a day, if properly organized. However, it was handled wrong from the very beginning. The instruction was just to do it, but it really did require a step-by-step process.

This is the scenario. We knew that we needed a virtual data center (VDC) setup, with one host and a VPN connection back to the local office. Setting up the VDC was easy, and so was the host, but we had problems with the VPN. A Point-to-Point Tunneling Protocol (PPTP) VPN was selected, and it was to connect back to a Netgear VPN Router. This took a week to get sorted, because a) we didn't know how to do it and b) the firewall was not set up correctly. Then a Remote Desktop Protocol (RDP) connection was required to the existing production host, but the password was saved in an RDP session on someone's desktop, and nobody knew what it was. We had to set up a screen-sharing session to gain access to the server and set up an account that could be used. This took another week, because several more people had to be involved, and time had to be scheduled to do these tasks. Next, the remote server had to be joined to the domain, which wasn't a big deal, but the VPN wasn't configuring DNS properly, and the remote server couldn't find the domain controller. It was at least another week before the job eventually got done.

How it should have played out was more like this:

- Setup a VDC.

- Install a server as a VM in the VDC.

- Establish a VPN from the new server to the local LAN.

- The VPN is a Microsoft-based PPTP connection to the Netgear VPN router.

- The Internet connection is over an asynchronous DSL line, but the MTU is non-standard. What type of circuit goes to the data center? Are there any incompatibilities between the two circuits that would prohibit a good VPN from working?

- Do some research on configuring the above VPN. Since the VDC server needs to join the domain, will DNS be propagated?

- Since access to the local server is required, who has the credentials? Do some research before you begin so that you can confirm the requirements.

- Generate a checklist of all the materials that are required before you start the task.

With a task like this, it's easy to spend about 20 minutes making a detailed list. Then spend a few days getting the information that you need from other people and gathering the requirements. More than likely, a few surprises may still arise. However, the odds are that you will get the job done within a day instead of it taking a month. It will help improve everyone else's work as well, because you won't have to bother them with questions during each step of the process.

Written Steps or High-Level Plan

Another one of my big beefs is to investigate in detail what has to be done, do the necessary research, and write it out. When you work in IT, some days can go by really fast, especially when you have a lot on your plate. If you're working on a big task with several steps, and those steps are documented, it's much easier to pick up where you left off when you're interrupted. Many people in other departments don't realize the number of complex tasks that IT may have at one time.

High-level plans allow you to think and plan ahead. If a new server is being built on an old hardware platform, it's a good idea to check for compatibility. Can Windows 2008 R2 run on an HP DL360 G5? Before you physically install the server, do your homework. Does the firmware need updating? There's nothing more frustrating than expecting to install a server today and then finding out the hardware isn't compatible. A high-level plan is not required for this, but written steps will do.

Major projects, on the other hand, do require high-level planning, such as looking for a new ERP system or planning to replace NC programming software. Before you start these types of projects, sit down and plan all the steps you think are required or the approach that is right for your business. For an ERP system, I would start by listing each department.

What is the process for each department? What are the inputs and outputs to each department? What kind of reports does each department require? It is best to involve the departments in this process to get accurate, detailed information. You can use the tools from *The Rational Manager* to create a decision spreadsheet for each department to track and compare.

I find that doing a demo of the software is good for a general gut feeling of how well it will work, but that certainly isn't as good as getting the software and trying to use it. It's very difficult to test an ERP system in a company, so a logical comparison of functionality is essential.

Sample decision spreadsheet.

Purchasing	Weight	ERP Software A	Score	Value	ERP Software B	Score	Value
Purchasing from multiple Job/Lots	3	Possible, but labour intensive	1	3	Yes, easy to do	8	24
Need accurate dates for required material, link to schedule	2	Yes, fully automated	8	16	Not possible	1	2
Need an easy way to email PO's	2	Interated to OWA	10	20	Manually download PDF	2	4
Once PO's are created easy to trace back to the Job/Lot (not just a flag that says linked)	3	Not an option	1	3	Fully integrated	9	27
Easy way to purchase from a BOM and track what was purchased and what is outstanding per job/lot (historical purchase)	2	No way	1	2	Yes can do	7	14
Total score				44			71

Within the decision spreadsheet above, list the software functionality under Purchasing. In the Weight column, enter a number between 1 and 3, which rates how important this functionality is to the business. The next column is for the first software choice and how it tackles each functionality. In the Score column, enter a number between 1 and 10, with 10 being the highest. Then in the Value column, simply multiply the Weight and the Score values. Do this for each type of software you want to compare. Sum up all the values, and you'll have a quantitative comparison to help with your decision process.

These kinds of charts should be included in your high-level plan for evaluating software. A plan of this scale would also have timelines and require some project planning. At the end of the day, if you think that you're spending way too much time updating a project management chart and not getting the job done, then you have a large scale project on your hands and need additional resources to help plan and execute it.

Do what is required to get the job done for the business—not too much, and not too little. If you feel like you're going around in circles, seek help. Keep senior management aware of the situation. Talk to other people in the company, like a mentor, about your project and its status. Sometimes, having a different perspective about what you're working on is all that's required to set things straight.

Checklists

I find checklists to be extremely useful. For day-to-day operations, IT personnel are assigned to specific areas. Each area should have a list of critical things that need to be checked.

Format your list on paper or keep an electronic copy. Break it up into sections for daily, weekly, monthly, and yearly tasks. A checklist can be used and filled in by staff, but it's mainly a reminder to make sure that tasks are getting done.

Review your checklist when you get to work each day. If you use it religiously, it can definitely help you maintain critical systems operations.

Sample checklist.

ADMINISTRATIVE TASKS

	DATE:						
	TASK	M	T	W	TH	F	COMMENT
Daily	Check ForeFront messages						
	Check the robocopy logs for remote locations						
	Disk space on erp-01 and fs-03 and database backups						Login to the server
	Check to see all Windows Terminal Servers are up.						WTSUsers.bat run the script
	Check backup drive status on storage servers						monitor icon on the desktop
	Check Exchange Queue Viewer, updates, DISK SPACE						...w/o sending NDRs, updates restart mornings
	Check all backups						run the script checker
	Check the updates on the Barracuda, SPAM filter						Advanced, firmware
	Check on generator during 9:45am-10:00am test startups						Winter time from 8:30am-9:00am
	server room check						Visually check UPS and power supplies
	remove dup tapes from the library						
	Backup ISA Firewall Policies						
	Review ISA 2006 Dashboard for alerts						
	Check App/System Log on ISA						

A sample checklist should include things like checking daily backups, offsite file sync, the generator, mail server, etc. I also recommend including the following: a) Monthly Windows updates and patches. b) Monthly reboots of Windows servers, typically after updates. If updates are skipped, still reboot the server. This is a best practice to keep systems running more stable. c) Daily checks to make sure anti-virus updates are still working. d) Weekly checks of event viewer logs on servers to look for critical errors. Even automated IT processes can fail, and so it's important to manually perform some basic checks to ensure the automation of processes continues to function properly.

Plan Before Doing

I know that I've already said this, but I can't stress it enough. IT is critical to the operation of your business, so you can't just leave things to chance. If you expect to get good, consistent results, you absolutely have to plan.

This chapter has shown you several tools that you can use to plan and organize IT operations—from day-to-day monitoring to individual task lists, decision-making tools, and even project planning. Use the right tool for the right job, and keep it simple.

6 Get Organized

Once your core structure has been put in place, meetings are being held, and plans are underway, it's time to gather information and use it to get organized.

Standards and Templates

A common problem is how to store and organize documents and data so that they can be retrieved when required.

The first standard that needs to be created is a template for all IT documentation. All documents should follow a standard format so that anyone can use them. Create a temple with a standard header that contains all the basic information.

Set up standard processes for common tasks. If the job is to install VMware ESXi on a server, and you do it quite frequently, create a template with standard questions that must be answered before starting. Ask things like 1) How much RAM is required? 2) How much usable disk is required? 3) How many processors? 4) What is the task the server will fulfill? 5) What is the network configuration? Establish a standard, and do it right the first time, so that you can repeat the process again in the future. Learn from your past experience and modify the standard to improve it.

Sample document template.

Document Title

OWNER / AUTHOR:

ENVIRONMENT:

IMPACTED ENTITIES:

REFERENCES:

DESCRIPTION:

CAUTIONARY NOTES:

COMMENTS:

BODY:

Another standard is to establish names for hardware, servers, desktop computers, printers, and scanners. Always stick to standard names so that it's easier to understand the purpose of the devices and where they are located. For example, with *division-shop-01*, division is the company name, shop is the department, and 01 is the first computer in the shop.

Create standards for IP addresses, and differentiate shop computers from office desktops and servers so that you can easily organize and track problems. Assign a range of IP addresses to accommodate the desired structure. For example, the shop floor could have a range like 172.16.100.x and be blocked from Internet access, while the office range of 172.16.20.x would not be blocked. Another option is to VLAN the shop floor on another LAN segment. This also makes it easier to create firewall rules based on departmental access. Ultimately, your IT team should decide and set the standards appropriate for your business.

Policies

You can reduce problems from re-occurring by defining policies. Establish policies based on feedback at meetings. For example, we wrote a policy regarding the installation of new software on Fridays. We had previously learned that we needed a way to prevent costly mistakes from happening. This policy helped provide a more stable network, reduce downtime, and lessen our stress level. Another policy we established was to never upgrade production servers to the most current release of Windows updates. Again, we learned these lessons after servers were damaged due to Windows updates. Don't get carried away and create a policy just for the sake of a policy, because there needs to be sound business logic behind each one.

Establish policies with the members of the IT department, and then guide your staff to use and enforce them. This is another way to encourage teamwork and give people a chance to get involved and have their say.

People outside of the IT department may think that policies where created to make their lives more difficult. They need to know that there are valid business reasons why polices exist. It's a good idea to seek opinions outside the IT department and adjust policies as necessary.

Lastly, make sure senior management has your back to enforce these policies.

Procedures

Procedures help maintain the quality and accuracy of repetitive tasks. For example, checklist procedures may include information about when and how you should install Windows core security patches. Enforce the procedures with IT staff, and let them know that their performance—that is, how well they stick to the standard procedures—will be rated.

Every new server or workstation that is built should follow the pre-established process and use the standard templates for documentation. Documents aren't written just for the person doing the install. They must be written so that any other IT person assigned to re-do the task can follow the steps and produce the same results.

This is the purpose of having procedures—to be able to successfully re-create a particular process. There are many times when this is important, like when you build a second server and want it set up identical to the first one, tracking the history of previous work, troubleshooting future problems, double-checking standards, and disaster recovery.

You can't manage a complex environment if you fly by the seat of your pants and try to remember everything that's been done. However, with a clearly documented process, it's easy to look back and follow the same process to resolve or complete a similar task.

Documentation

You can realize the importance of documentation when you liken it to going to your family doctor when you're sick. Every visit is logged, detailed notes are taken, and the sum of all this becomes your medical history. Over the course of your life, you have a record of important health information, like medications that you're allergic to so that your doctor doesn't prescribe it to you in the future. Having good documentation is extremely important for your IT environment as well.

Using the documentation procedure and templates that are defined by the IT department, clearly write down everything that you do so that everyone can read it. Surprisingly, a lot of people don't see the need to document an install process, but I firmly believe that is essential. It helps you repeat a process or recover from a problem, plus it's simply good business practice. There are many different ways to accomplish the same task, but the documentation will let you know how something was done and why.

Make sure to create network maps to document the location of all desktop computers, thin clients, servers, and network switches. This will help track down problems and troubleshoot faster. If you remotely support users, it will also help identify the computer in question. A network map should have sufficient detail to identify all network data port numbers, computer types, and names connected to the port. As the network is updated, make sure to write down any changes.

Typically, I break documents up by type and create folders appropriately, such as Network, Windows, and UNIX. For example, a server document would be stored under ITDocs\division \windows\server\server-name. All documents required to build this particular server would reside here.

Storage Structure

Once your procedures have been created, you need to properly save and file your documentation.

Before creating the folder structure for storing documents, review the storage process with the other members of the IT department in case they have input or suggestions. This is important, because everyone has to use the system the same way so that it's easy to retrieve all the documentation that's created. Larger organizations may even consider a storage system, such as SharePoint, where they can save their documentation.

System Documentation
Revision Number 1

Division-fs-04 Install

OWNER / AUTHOR: Dave Collings

ENVIRONMENT: Storage server

IMPACTED ENTITIES:

REFERENCES: This server was created to replace the old Lacie server, 10 Terabytes of network attached disk.

DESCRIPTION: Install of a synology Storage array

CAUTIONARY NOTES:

COMMENTS:

BODY:

1. Physically connect the server to the network.
2. Balance power cables across 2 UPS's
3. Reused the same network cable as the old storage server
4. Reused the same IP address of 172.16.26.25
5. Download the DSM software from Synology's web site.
6. Use the Synology Assistant application to install the OS and set up the default RAID array.
7. Connect using a Web Browser, 172.16.26.25:5000, login: admin Password: xxxx
8. Control Panel, Directory Services, Join a Domain.
9. Set up a "Data"shared folder from the control panel, under shared folder
10. Under Control Panel, Notifications. Set them up to email to -admins

Senior Management Support

Keeping business continuity is important. In order for IT to have the necessary responsibility and authority to carry out its duties, they must have support from senior management. Senior management and IT need to work together, with open and honest communication. It's imperative that long-term plans, such as 5-year goals, are discussed so that IT can prepare itself for the future.

If future plans indicate that the company is going to be growing or expanding exponentially or purchasing new manufacturing equipment, this impacts IT operations. The infrastructure needs to be designed with growth and flexibility in mind.

IT and senior management jobs are not interchangeable. They are simply two different factions. However, it is essential that they mutually understand and respect their roles and keep the lines of communication open.

Meetings

Weekly IT meetings are effective for keeping staff on track and focused. During the course of the week, encourage members of the IT team to write down issues on a whiteboard so that they can be openly discussed and resolved.

Meetings are a great way to communicate and keep up on what's happening, but don't meet just for the sake of meeting. If a particular topic is discussed, make sure all relevant people are there. Always prepare an agenda if you are the one calling the meeting, and always follow up with the meeting minutes. Structure meetings appropriately so that everyone's voice is heard. Keep the meeting start time and duration to a schedule. Time is important, so don't waste it.

Managers, particularly in small organizations, should consider joining other departmental meetings to see what's coming up in different areas of the business. Don't wait for people to come to you—be proactive and look for business problems so that you can help solve them. Structure your resources appropriately, and plan based on the overall corporate requirements.

Allocating Resources

IT needs to deliver projects and tasks on time. It's important to structure the resources within the IT department to focus on different aspects. Each IT person needs to be responsible for at least one area. For example, one person could be responsible for desktops, and another person could be responsible for servers. The person responsible for desktops could cover uptime, rolling out new applications, software updates, and be the main point of contact for desktop problems. The person responsible for servers could also cover network and end-point protection. This is the operation side of the business. The other side is growing the business, like adding new functions and features to enhance performance. If the business is small, additional projects can be added to the same staff member. You can also hire outside contractors to help or perform special tasks that require a focused skill set.

Use the weekly IT meetings to make sure people within the group are communicating. The network people need to communicate with the workstation people regarding tasks that are reliant on one another. Review task and project status and completion times, plus staff workloads. Are tasks and projects getting complete within a reasonable amount of time? Are people struggling with issues? Is extra help required to solve difficult problems? This is your chance to help the IT team and bring in additional resources if required.

Updates

How do you keep the rest of the business up to speed on tasks and projects? This is part of the open communication between the IT team and the rest of the business. Make sure to follow up on tasks that have been discussed at meetings. Continuous feedback for ongoing projects is necessary. People outside of the IT department, from senior management to end users, also need to be kept in the loop. With a small team of IT people, this can be a challenge. Encourage members of the IT team to focus on getting information and providing feedback. This keeps senior management informed, lets users know that their problems are getting resolved, and helps IT understand the business better.

During your weekly meeting, discuss the interaction between IT staff and end users, including feedback about user satisfaction. The manager of the IT department needs to support the IT staff *and* the users. For example, you maybe need to send a brief email to the corporation to deal with the progress of certain projects. Ultimately, you have to find a balance by providing a good solution that is still acceptable to the business. Don't forget that the needs of many people outweigh the needs of a few.

Surveys

A good way to stay abreast of new business challenges and problems is to get feedback from employees using a survey. Keep your surveys short and ask open-ended questions. They are designed to gather useful information, not answer a bunch of structured questions. Most importantly, don't overdo them, because people can easily get frustrated.

Surveys should target two areas: operational issues and business issues. Operational issues inform the IT department of any problems that require attention, like a computer that always crashes, the Internet dragging, and certain Internet sites that won't load. Business issues cover broader topics, like the capability of the existing ERP system and possible business shortcomings.

A survey can also be done informally, like in a meeting or one-on-one discussions. Gather the information and decide what can be done to improve things. Work them into tasks lists for the IT team. Each person should have some small areas that they are responsible for.

Review the results of the survey with the IT department and senior management if required.

Organized Conclusions

In this chapter, we have walked through how to use various tools to improve the operation of the department. Standards, polices, procedures, and documentation help create common ways to communicate. Meetings and management support allow IT to get involved in the business, communicate status, and improve the overall efficiency. Don't isolate IT from the rest of the business. Remember, keep it simple, and plan before doing.

Chapter 7

7 Storage

Storage is a huge topic, but this chapter only covers it briefly. Small businesses don't need a large Storage Area Network (SAN) for local storage. In these cases, a Network Attached Storage (NAS) will work just fine.

Windows ACLs

An Access Control Level (ACL) is a list of permissions attached to an object. It specifies which users or system processes are granted access to objects and what operations are allowed on given objects. Each entry in a typical ACL specifies a subject and an operation. For instance, if a file has an ACL that contains (George, delete), this would give George permission to delete the file.

Having Windows ACL fully supported on the storage server allows detailed granular security permissions that can be applied to files and folders. This is ideal for breaking up storage by departments adding fine controls. However, try to avoid applying individual user-level permissions onto folders and files.

The best approach I found was to define departmental folders, and then put users in groups that give them full access to their departmental folders. Other departments can be granted read access.

For example, you may have some users who belong to a group called Engineering. You can create a folder called Engineering and then apply security that allows that group full access. Users who belong to the Production or the NC Programming group could have read-level access, allowing them to view shared files only. This would protect the Engineering data from other people within the organization possibly tampering with it.

Storage Structure

One of the biggest benefits of storage structure is that you can more easily store and retrieve files. Create a standard and teach it to the entire company so that everyone is on the same page.

Within the shared network drive, created folders for each department and give the respective members full read/write access. These will become the departmental storage share areas. Each department should determine how to structure the data in each folder. Meetings can be held with departments to optimally structure their files. Come up with a format agreement, and then document it. Each department will be responsible for maintaining their own storage structure based on how they work.

UNIX Support

Do you still need to support those older UNIX workstations for legacy data? Windows Storage Server still maintains Network File System (NFS) support, and it is possible to share out storage on Windows for those UNIX workstations.

If older UNIX workstations are still around, make sure NFS is still supported. In the early days of shared storage, costs were extremely high. It was very common to build your own storage system on lower-cost UNIX systems and then use Samba to join an Active Directory domain and share files and print services to Windows computers. At the time, permissions were limited to UNIX, owner, group, and everyone. Windows ACLs offered much more flexibly and security. To this day, it is still a valid option to use a UNIX server, free BSD, and ZFS file systems. However, it requires some comfort level with UNIX, which many people don't have, because there are quality low-cost alternatives like Synology and Qnap that offer full Windows ACL support. If data integrity is one of your highest priorities, a ZFS file system may be a good option to consider.

For reliable production storage, vendors like HP and Dell have nice products based on the Windows Storage Server OS. These devices work well, but you still should make sure that you have a well-tested backup and recovery process with your storage servers.

SharePoint

SharePoint is a very powerful and flexible file content management tool that's used to securely share documents. For smaller operations, like engineering firms, first consider the priorities of your business. An engineering firm may levitate more towards a Project Lifecycle Management (PLM) system, which has its own complications and issues. I'll discuss that next.

SharePoint may be a valid option if there are no constraints on data management. There are options to modify SharePoint with workflow functions, plus documents can be shared to people inside and outside of the business. SharePoint also can be hosted by Microsoft or installed on a local server. Research your business requirements, and decide what's right for you.

PLM

A PLM system is software for managing engineering data. High-end systems have hooks into the engineering design software that help automate and improve the design to manufacture process. While engineers design in the CAD system, the PLM system can be configured in such a way that bill of materials (BOMs) can be automatically generated and then fed to the ERP systems for purchasing and manufacturing needs.

The purpose of a PLM system is to manage the entire lifecycle of the product, from inception to manufacturing, and even through the purchasing process. For example, engineering could release data to the shop floor with instructions about how to manufacture a particular product. Data can be structured with the PLM system to flow through the company, and vendors can have access to the PLM system to download data for subcontract work.

PLMs can be very big, complex, and costly. The challenge with most manufacturers is that their customers tend to have their own PLM systems and expect their vendors (you, the manufacturer) to use them. This is great for the customer, but it isn't so good for your manufacturing process. If your firm wants a PLM system, it has to be compatible with the customer. Data has to be imported from the customer's system, worked on, and then exported back into the customer's system. The design must follow the customer's standards precisely, or the data will be rejected. Take time to study and plan if this is something that you are considering.

A PLM is not something to rush into. Done correctly and with sufficient resources, it can vastly improve your business processes. However, be forewarned that there is a cost to maintain beyond the licenses of the software. To be compatible with the customer, you need to stay on compatible versions of the PLM systems. So, you must have the resources to maintain this, whether they are onsite or subcontracted.

Business Process

Understanding the business requirements and associated costs to maintain the IT systems is very important. It's a fine balance to keep the operation running and being able to add new business processes. Senior management must understand this and recognize the cost and complexity by adding tools like SharePoint or a PLM. This needs to be part of the business plan and future budgets so that you can sustain the systems.

There are simple ways to get some of the benefit of a PLM system by having a standard way to release data. In the past, I've set up a Release_To_Production folder. Engineering would release data in standard, read-only format to the shop floor. The shop floor could easily retrieve it by knowing and following the standard. The standard should follow the business flow within your company. A good place to start is by defining *customer \ job or design \ <components or structure of the job>*. Be as detailed as required to uniquely define all the types of data and how they are to be organized. Establish standards with each department and publish them. The individual department should take ownership and work to improve the standards and share them across the company.

Compiling a manual storage system and flow of business documents can establish the groundwork for a PLM system. In other words, analyze and figure out which system will work best, and then move it to an automated process that can be further enhanced with a PLM.

Future of Storage

Technology is forever changing and evolving. Make sure that you always have a process or standard to follow. Technology can enhance your processes and make your job easier, but don't rely on it to solve your problems.

There's a lot of talk about the future of software design data centers and storage. Keep an eye on the trends of technology and tools, but don't implement something that will eventually lead to a dead end situation. For example, if server virtualization is the trend, it makes sense to use it, because 10 physical servers are more costly to purchase and maintain then 10 virtual servers on the same physical hardware.

Take a look at Nutanix: http://www.nutanix.com. This company offers centrally managed software that's fully configured, provides failover, redundancy, and is easy to expand. This is how large companies like Google, Facebook, and Apple expand and grow their environments so quickly. It may not work for every company or service, but it's the way things are going.

I've evaluated storage arrays, like EMC and Netapp, which are both powerful and complex storage solutions. Netapp is good example of a "best of breed" system. There's nothing wrong with it, but it can often do more than a small business requires. Also, some functions require you to be comfortable with the command-line interface. EMC seems to do a better job at packaging things so that it's easier for the average user, which makes it a better fit for a small business.

Windows Storage Servers from vendors like Dell and HP are great options for SMBs. From my experience, they aren't as reliable as systems from

EMC or Netapp, but they may be totally fine for your business. Make sure that you investigate and design a system that is suitable for your business needs.

For smaller businesses, it's very easy to house all your servers in one physical box, including the storage. Build a fault tolerance hardware platform and virtualize the required servers within storage, email, and ERP. I have done this with remote offices, and it works great. Back up images of each server to low-cost NAS drives. That way, any server can easily be restored.

Also, don't forget about the cloud as a possible place to store data. In the end, keep it simple, and do what's right for the growth of the business.

Chapter 8

8 Backups

Backups are crucial for every organization. It can be very costly to implement a full-blown backup system, but there are several things that you can do to keep it simple.

Keep it Simple

In the old days, costly tape backups were the only way to handle the massive amounts of data an engineering firm could produce. You also needed tape libraries and software to manage the databases and tapes. Today, we don't have to rely on these technologies as much. Low-cost disks and the cloud are viable alternatives.

To keep costs down, utilize Windows backups for all production servers. Script, schedule, and run backups at various times throughout the week. Every single server needs a complete image backup onto disk. Create scripts to automate the process and store the backups in logically arranged file systems.

Backup your systems (such as database servers for ERP) and mail servers (such as Exchange) nightly.

Most small business databases can easily be exported within one hour to hard disk. Again, use disk space on older slower Windows Storage Servers or low-cost NAS (like Synology) disk arrays. This is a very simple and clean way to manage all backups. No costly software or licenses are required, and all are based on Robocopy and Windows backup. The same logic can be performed at remote sites, and then use Robocopy to pull data across the WAN on weekends and quiet times.

At offsite locations, tape or disaster recovery backups and more management control may be required, depending on how much data you have. If you're using the cloud, you may need software like Robocopy or rsync to backup and synchronize the data, because most backups are retained on local hard drives that are relatively inexpensive. Data storage in the cloud, on the other hand, can be expensive. You really only need to synchronize one set of the most current full backups to the cloud. It's not necessary to keep three years of data there.

You can easily create a few Windows scripts to automate and monitor your backups to a hard drive. Backups should be included on an IT staff's daily checklist. Monitoring the backup process only takes five or 10 minutes each. The automation process should also be monitored to make sure everything is working properly. The IT staff can create a scripted dashboard that will show high-level automation at a glance.

Don't overcomplicate backups or pay extensive license fees for software. The money you save by not purchasing backup software can be put towards a new machine to make more widgets. In manufacturing, this is what it's all about. IT needs to support the business of making widgets, so keep it simple. Use built-in Windows functions Volume Shadow Services (VSS) for daily incremental backups.

An automated tape drive unit and one license of backup software can manage backups that are longer term. The only system that requires an offsite backup is the local server, which stores all the backup data. USB attached drives can be used in place of an automated tape, but it all depends on the business requirement and the amount of data to be backed up. Full weekly backups saved to tape or disk are kept for one month. Of that monthly backup, the last week of the month is kept for three years.

This method is very low-cost and simple. Alternately, the tape drive backup can be switched with cloud storage services to reduce the effort in managing physical tapes. Simply synchronize one full set of weekly backups to the provider.

Easy Recovery

Backups must be easy to manage, run, and recover. For day-to-day incremental file recoveries, use VSS. If the primary storage is on Windows, use the build-in Windows' products. This covers all the daily files that people need, plus it's extremely easy and fast to use. Right-click on the file to recover past versions. This is typically good for three months worth of backups, with two shadow copies configured per day. However, if you loose the production server and recover it, the volume shadows will be gone. So, to keep those backups around, run a nightly Robocopy script that makes a full copy of your production data to another server. This backup server can be older and slower. I like to use low-cost NAS servers with big data disks. Speed is not as critical as capacity.

For Windows Storage Servers, run nightly scripted backups to image the entire OS on the server to a locally attached external hard drive. In case a storage server fails to boot, it takes about two hours to recover a storage server from an image. Test this and document the procedure for recovery.

Also, keep a full set of bootable flash drives for every server you have, in every OS flavor. In case any server has a major failure, you should have new power supplies and hard drives in stock to copy the backup image to a new USB-attached drive. Attach this to the downed server using the bootable USB drive, boot the system to one of the Windows bootable flash drives, and restore from the backup image. This will give you a full restore of a server in under two hours from complete failure. There is no additional cost of software or licensing to do this. It's simple, low cost, and works very well.

If faster recover times are required as a business objective, create a set of disk-to-disk copies of the operating system bootable drives. Schedule this to be done at regularly intervals. It's also important to keep the drives up to fairly current patch levels.

Server Images

From my experience, I find it best to image the entire server at least once a week. If a disaster strikes, the server is, at most, one week behind. Incremental data backups will restore the server to within one day. I've used this method for several years. It's a robust solution for a small business and keeps things simple and cost-effective.

Server images also need to be copied offsite or to tape in case of a major emergency.

Lastly, it's only a matter of time before mechanical hard drives fail. The same can be said for power supplies. Be prepared, test your disaster recovery service, and keep critical spare parts for servers.

Production Data

Daily production data is kept on Windows servers with VSS enabled, and a complete copy is replicated onto a secondary server. In a worst-case scenario, the secondary server could be reconfigured and brought online as the main storage server for virtually instant recover.

Disaster recovery is something you plan for but don't plan to use. In production, I've used the storage server disaster recovery processes depicted above on three occasions. Each time, they worked successfully. What I write here is not fantasy or proposed. It has all been used and works well in a production environment.

Disaster Recovery

Disaster recovery is essential, along with having a generator backing up the servers in the IT room. In bad weather, there's a greater chance of power outages, dips, and spikes. Make sure your computer systems, servers, and desktops are protected with a battery backup. When the power goes off in the IT room, the batteries will take the initial load until the generator is up to speed. When selecting a generator, make sure that it's capable of powering computers and able to run behind the computer Uninterruptible Power Supply (UPS).

In event of a major system failure, use the server backup images to restore damaged servers and data backups to restore the data.

Another step I take to speed recovery is having a few old hypervisor servers handy. In recent versions of Microsoft hyperv, it's now possible to create replica servers. For critical servers, ERP, email, etc., replicate to a backup server. In a worst-case scenario, if recovery is too long, spin up the backup server and continue. Schedule some downtime to rebuild the original production server and then move your data back over.

Along with your image backups, make sure you completely document how each server was built. If there are problems with the recovery of a server, documentation can help.

Cloud

In simple terms, the cloud refers to software and services that run on the Internet and are hosted by a provider, as opposed to running on your computer or hosted on your local site. Instead of writing the backup to a local device, the backup is redirected to a cloud service provider like Amazon Web Services (AWS).

This has been a big trend the last several years. However, before you move to the cloud for backups, perform a cost justification study. Compare this against the traditional way of doing backups and the hybrid way, which is a combination of local hard disk and disaster recovery to the cloud. I believe that the hybrid way is the sweet spot, because you just need to synchronize a copy of the weekly backups to the cloud, and it's a lot easier and cheaper then sending tapes offsite.

Chapter 9

9 Centrally Managed

Centrally managed systems provide a lot of central control and vastly simplify the efforts of system admins. The ability to manage and make a change in one place that affects all computers or a group of computers is essential, because it's a big time saver. Make your life easier, empower the admins, plan, and think logically.

Push Installs

You need some powerful tools for updating applications and pushing out new applications to desktops, but don't go out and buy expensive management tools. Historically, I've found that management tools take considerable time and effort to maintain. A much simpler approach is to keep desktop hardware as consistent as possible and create standard software images that can be pushed out. This creates a solid base where updates can be pushed on top of the core images.

Using Sysinternals PsTools, you can install almost any application. With high-end engineering applications, there are always complex steps that need to be performed to complete the install. A script in Windows batch language or PowerShell can fully automate almost any install procedure. Once you've created a script, you can schedule it to run at any time —day, night, or weekend. Use PsTools within batch files to fully automate and log the install process.

Here is a batch file that will install Siemens UG NX 6.0:

@echo on

rem installs UG NX 6.0 64 bit, set software install from and install to locations
red the path for the NX install code
set INST=\ \fs-03\Software\Unigraphics \NX6_64\nx060\UGS Nx 6.0.msi
red the path for the NX documentation
set INST_DOC=\ \fs-03\Software\Unigraphics \NX6_64\ \win64\ugdoc060\UGS NX 6.0 Documentation.msi

rem install locations on the workstation

```
set INSTALL_DIR=C:\Program Files\UGS\NX 6.0
set UGII_BASE_DIR=C:\Program Files\UGS\NX 6.0

echo "set env variables use NX6 config locations"
setx /m HOMEDRIVE C:\
setx /m HOMEPATH C:\TEMP\
setx /m UGII_SDI_OUTPUT_DIR C:\TEMP\
setx /m UGII_SDI_OVERRIDE_HOME C:\TEMP\
setx /m UGII_SDI_SERVER_CFG_DIR \\ENV\UG\NX6\PLOT\
setx /m UGII_SITE_DIR \\ENV\UG\NX6\SITE\
setx /m UGII_LOAD_OPTIONS \\ENV\UG\NX\load_options.def

echo make sure c:\temp exists on the computer being installed
mkdir c:\temp
```

```
icacls c:\temp /grant users:(f) /t /c /q


rem
echo Installation UG Begin


echo "install NX6"
msiexec /qn+ /L*v c:\temp\ug6_install.log /i
"%INST%" ADDLOCAL="all"
INSTALLDIR="%INSTALL_DIR%"
LICENSESERVER=28000@lic-01


echo Install doc Begin
msiexec /qn+ /i "%INST_DOC%"
INSTALLDIR="%INSTALL_DIR%"


echo Install update 5 for NX6, copy and run locally or
map a drive


net use Z: \\fs-03\drive1 /USER:<Domain>
\administrator <password> /PERSISTENT:YES
```

cd Z:\Software\Unigraphics
\NX6_64\dvdrom0605_03\ugs_update0605

Z:

ugs_update.bat /d

cd Z:\Software\Unigraphics
\NX6_64\605_03_mp05

ugs_update.bat

C:

cd c:

net use Z: /delete

The batch file above will install Siemens UG NX 6 unattended on the machine it is intended for. To automate the process, run the following script:

psexec @%1 -u <Domain>\administrator -p <Password> -c C:\install\UG6\install-UG-NX6_64.bat

Give the script above a name like Install_UG. From a command line, type the following:

Install_UG <file_name>

The *file_name* consists of a text file of all the computers that need to be installed. The line *pressed @ %1* calls the file with all the computers to be installed. You can script the command to run at anytime of the day or night by using Windows Scheduler.

For more detailed information on PsExec, visit the following Microsoft website: https:// technet.microsoft.com/en-ca/sysinternals/ bb897553.aspx

VNC to Desktops

Admins can quickly and easily connect to a users desktop and assist them with problems by installing VNC on all workstations. Some machines, like Wyse terminals, already have VNC built in. When users are unsure of their computer name, but you know where they sit, use a network map to identify their computer. Connect to the computer via VNC so that you can investigate and solve their problem. This gives the admin full access to the existing desktop for troubleshooting, and there are no addition costs or licensing fees required. No extra service needs to be purchased for this to work.

This is a much better approach than visiting the desktop of the problem computer. Centralized management tools make the most of administrators' time, because a lot of issues can be resolved faster and easier remotely. Having said that, there are occasions when it is necessary to visit end users and understand what's going on. This is the discretion of the admin solving the problem.

Terminal Servers and VDI

Terminal servers have been around since the late 1990s, and they've advanced over time to become mature, stable products. For kiosks and users that run the same applications, general office users, accountants, purchasing agents, and receptionists—all of their desktops can be hosted on a terminal server instead of a desktop PC. One properly configured server can easily support 25 or more users. The desktops are thin client-based, such as Dell WYSE terminals, and connect to the terminal server with RDP.

As a result, there is one computer to maintain as opposed to 25. Also, the terminal server can be physical or virtual, which eliminates many hardware issues. WYSE thin clients are centrally managed, boot over TFTP, and pick up where to get their configuration files from DNS. Multiple terminal servers can also be used and clustered together for some level of fault tolerance.

Keep spare WYSE terminals on a shelf, ready to go. If a production unit fails, swap it out immediately and update the network maps to indicate a change. Also, enter a ticket in your ticketing system to indicate that there was a problem and what was done to fix it. As a side note, it's very important to keep your system documentation up to date with changes. Other system admins are working on solving problems too, so this helps keep them informed of what work has already been done.

VDI is a direct replacement for desktop computers. This is a process where a virtual computer is created for each person on the hypervisor server instead of sharing access to the same server in the case of a terminal server. For power users, VDI is the way to go, because it's one step beyond terminal servers and a bit more complex. The same WYSE terminals can be used to connect to a VDI computer over RDP.

A big advantage of terminal servers is that, by default, users can't install anything. This is a bonus, because it decreases the chance that viruses and malware will cause damage.

Software Config

Having different config files distributed on individual desktop computers is complex and hard to manage without some sort of central control. Centrally manage your software configurations whenever possible. For example, PowerMILL is used for NC programming so that users all share the same feed and speed tables. In this case, have one centrally located tool library on a server, and allow every desktop that's configured to use it. The configuration file that tells PowerMILL where to look should also be centrally located.

It's also possible to have one set of master config files and have it copied out to all desktop computers. Some applications, like Lemoine RTM, work and perform best when all the libraries are copied locally to each computer. In small environments, you can create a simple Robocopy or login script to do this. Larger organizations should investigate alternative options, like Apache Zookeeper and Cassandra, for synchronizing data and metadata across multiple computers or servers.

Again, keep it simple for your business. Find the tool that does the job and is easy to setup, use, and maintain.

Login Scripts

Some processes are easier to manage with login scripts than Active Directory. If the environment is complex, with various types of application and storage servers, login scripts can help. This is especially true if your environment is a mixture of Windows and UNIX, because scripting allows some flexibility to work around UNIX limited permissions. These centrally ran scripts, configured to run at login from Active Directory, may copy out small config files, set default printers, map network drives, run registry edits, etc. They are great for terminal server users as logins and can be easily customized for each person, depending on the department or role.

Like the previous example, a login script was used for RTM to copy library files to the local computer at each login, which ensures that the files are current.

Active Directory

Pretty much every company uses Active Directory. It's an awesome tool to gain central management control over your network. Drives can also be mapped here, but I mostly use Active Directory to control the environment. Some other good uses of Active Directory include disabling users from installing software, clearing temporary folders on logout, setting desktop or Windows preferences, and establishing profile caching preferences for terminal services performance.

Get feedback from users about their preferred settings so that you can provide the optimum positive end-user experience.

No Fancy Management Software

This is one area that constantly needs to be questioned and challenged. There are lots of great tools out there that will help manage your environment, such as AIK (for imaging computers) and System Center Essentials. Analyze what's best for your environment. Write your own scripts and build (or purchase) your own tools. The tools you purchase will require regular updates and continuous configuration to keep them current and functioning. Custom install scripts, on the other hand, are very easy to create and manage.

Ultimately, do what's right for your environment —plan, test, price it out, and keep it simple. Question and challenge how your environment is set up and running, because what is right and works today may not be what is right and works for your business tomorrow.

Chapter 10

10 Performance

Every company would like lightning-speed response time and super fast performance. However, there are business limitations that don't allow unlimited budgets and resources. So, you need to know your business priorities.

Know Your Environment

If you take the time to really get to know your business and the environment, you'll be more sensitive to performance and what you may need. I discuss this in greater detail in Chapter 12, so you can acquire a good understanding of what work takes place in each department, the computer requirements, the flow of work through the business, and possible bottlenecks.

For example, engineering desktops for a manufacturer of very large molds require more and faster memory. Improved boot times and application load times will be enhanced with SSD hard disks. Network connections must be 1 GB back to the IT room. A high-end Nvidia graphics card is required to annotate CAD models quick and efficiently. Access to storage servers is critical, as engineers typically have large assemblies to open, which can easily be 800+ MB of data. Terminal servers should also have 1 GB network connections, since they are shared by multiple users. Desktop thin clients run RDP, so 100 MB network speed is more than enough.

Design your network so that the links to desktops are slower than the links to the servers and core switches. If the desktop is connected at 1 GB, the core switches and servers should be connected at 10 GB. Theoretically, you could have 10 users pulling data just as fast as one simultaneously, with no degradation. Based on the number of users you have and their performance needs, you'll have to perform sizing if new switches are required. Once you've determined the type of switches you need to buy, work with the vendor to select the final product and configuration for optimal performance.

Monitoring

There are many reasons why monitoring is essential. It lets you know if servers and services are performing as desired—and if there are problems, it helps you troubleshoot and resolve them. Monitoring is similar to preventative maintenance, like changing the oil in your car. There are several tools available, including Sysinternals for monitoring performance, plus Filemon, Regmon, and Wireshark for monitoring and troubleshooting problems. The combination of these applications together can provide a ton of information.

One time, I experienced a problem on terminal services, where some rogue processes were consuming 100% of all the CPU cores available on the server. With the monitoring tools listed above, I was able to find processor threads that were causing the problems. The culprit application was discovered and removed.

Automation is a huge bonus for IT, but when it fails, a downstream process may get affected. Over time, with Windows updates and data growth, processes can take longer to run. If two automated processes are scheduled to run, one right after the other, they may eventually fail. For example, with one ERP system, a custom database was created to gather time and allocation of man-hours to machines. This process was scheduled to run at 4:45 AM, and database backups where scheduled to run just before at 4:30 AM. Over time, the backups took longer than 15 minutes, which interfered with the schedule to generate man-hours for machines.

An IT person's daily checklist needs to include the monitoring of automated processes so that they continue to run properly. In the case of the ERP system, monitoring the automated processes showed that the number of man-hours was failing to calculate properly. The automation times were adjusted so that everything could run on schedule.

Here's a good tip: When you're building systems or servers that require process automation, keep a separate document that lists all automation efforts. This is a big help for troubleshooting problems or adjusting automation schedules. Also, if possible, try to keep automated processes running on one server. This will simplify where to look for problems.

Network

Network performance is a foundation component, like the foundation of your house. If the foundation fails, everything on top of the foundation will collapse.

Cisco makes a nice, reliable switch, but Dlink has switches that perform just as well, with nearly the same reliability but 1/3 the cost. Use Cisco on the edges or boundaries of the network where reliability and performance are most critical and Dlink in all other locations. Keep it simple and cost effective.

Typically, I always plan and keep my network fairly current, which helps me avoid having many network issues. When planning equipment purchases, never put in what just works for today. Plan for five years down the road, and make sure the switches have sufficient bandwidth. Even in a medium-sized engineering firm that pushes around large amounts of data, core switches should have at least 10 GB interconnects.

The same applies for network cabling. Don't cheap out on low cost cabling. Do it right from the very beginning. Put the best in you can get and what makes sense for the business.

Workstations

Based on years of trial and error, here are my thoughts about workstations. In a manufacturing environment, users that have workstations are typically power users. These workstations tend to generate lots of heat, because they run fairly hard for at least 8 hours a day, 5 days a week. Some shop floor workstation can even run 24x7. High-end graphics cards produce a lot of excess heat as well. Remember that these computers will sit in place for three years at least, sucking up dirt and dust, which can clog the computers and causes them to heat up even more. More than likely, you won't have the resources to clean these computers out on a regular basis. So, help extend their life by getting a small tower so air can pass through them. A decent tower will cost an additional $80.00 on average.

If you have dedicated workstations that run analysis 24x7, do not use SSD hard drives. Stick to mechanical hard drives with the fastest memory possible. SSDs will most likely burnout within one year, plus they have a write ratio, which means that data can be written to them only so many times before they fail. These drives continue to improve, and monitoring/maintenance software can extend their life. However, until the technology matures, stick to mechanical drives for heavy use. Even with mini towers, the memory and at least one power supply will likely fail over a two or three year period.

Treat shop floor workstations that run CAM applications the same way that you treat office computers. Shop floors typically have more dirt and dust that clog the computers. A bigger case will help with airflow and keep the contents cooler.

Terminal Servers

Terminal servers, when sized correctly and load balanced, can easily support 25 users or more. In fact, I prefer to size the servers for 25 users and introduce a second or third server for load balancing and redundancy. Try to keep the server on newer hardware with lots of memory. Newer hardware typically has more threads per core, which boosts overall user performance. The best way to find out how to size the server for performance is to test it out. Build a server, get some users on it, load it down, and watch how it performs.

Internet

Good Internet performance is a must. Size the connection for the business. For example, manufacturing facilities usually deal with large files, and adequate performance is required to move them around. If there are VPNs to other facilities and to customers for PLM clients, these also need to be considered.

An IT person's checklist should include the responsibility of testing the Internet speed with the help of a speed test application, like the one available on http://www.speedtest.net. That same person should also monitor the Internet bandwidth at various times of the day to make sure the company has enough bandwidth to perform optimally and figure out if there are peek usage times. The firewall or ISP may also provide some reports that show usage patterns. It's very important to know if you have sufficient capacity on your data lines.

Discuss Internet performance during your weekly meeting. Are any users complaining? This is something that you need to be on top of. Users complaining of performance issues will impact their work. Keep the door open and listen to the needs of the business.

WAN, Remote Offices

If you're responsible for remote sites and VPN interconnectivity, keep an ear open for complaints, especially if these offices are located in countries where the communication infrastructure is not as good as North America (for example, Mexico or Indonesia).

Make sure someone's checklist includes the task of monitoring these remote office communications and reporting any known issues. It's pretty easy to do a daily speed test to make sure data is getting across these WANs in a reasonable amount of time. A ping test for latency is a good idea to incorporate if there are any VoIP lines for video conferencing running across the VPN. These types of communications are sensitive to the timely delivery of network packets so that communication is not interrupted.

Extend thin clients to remote locations where possible. If the services can be hosted from one central location, that's even better. However, if user complaints and testing indicate poor performance, serving thin clients across a WAN may not be feasible. Communicate with other departments and users, and then make the best, most cost-effective decision for the business to get the desired results.

Chapter 11, Part 2

11 Lean IT

In Part 1, we covered some of the core fundamentals. Now, let's leverage that information to make things work to your advantage in Part 2. I'll provide a bit more detail in this section and offer more examples to explain things more clearly.

What is Lean IT?

Lean IT is the extension of lean manufacturing. The goal of lean IT is to eliminate waste, which is work done that adds little or no value to a product or service. Some areas of waste include poor customer service, lost business, decline in user productivity, and higher operating costs. Lean IT is still an emerging industry, as it's relatively new.

How Does Lean IT Help?

Let's take a look at how some of the things I have learned and implemented impact the waste in IT. For the sake of comparison, I reference the type of waste Wikipedia has pointed out for lean IT (https://

en.m.wikipedia.org/wiki/
Lean_IT#Types_of_Waste_in_Lean_IT).

Defects: Established IT polices are in places to prevent unauthorized system changes or updates. The same applies to development efforts. Development environments are created and tests are performed to minimize the amount of defective code that's released to the production environment. IT employees are measured by how well they adhere to the policies, procedures, and standards.

Overproduction: This is where the IT department needs to really know the business. Plug into departmental meetings. Keep senior management involved with key initiatives in IT. Don't do things that are not of use to the business.

Waiting: Know the business and the priorities. Equipment that directly affects production has the highest priority. In the case of the shop floor PC failure, spare PCs are kept on hand, and a goal is set to have shop floor PCs swapped out within an hour if the existing PC can't be repaired.

Non-value Added Processing: This is a constant battle. I've never implemented a help desk in a small manufacturing business. Instead, I trained people how to do their job. I learned early on that if users don't get the answer they want, they try to go around the system. So, design a system that's flexible. IT staff are made aware of the situation within the business and are trained using standards, policies, and procedures that reflect the business objectives. These policies and processes should be questioned and reviewed on a regular basis and updated when required.

Transportation: Build a solid base, centralize (centrally manage), and create push tools for installing software. Utilize VNC to remotely manage computers and save support personal from visiting every person with a problem.

Inventory: This is a tricky one, because an inventory of parts is required to keep systems up and running. Build a simple visual inventory system so that you don't waste time looking for spare parts. Stay closely involved with the business, and tune the checklists to monitor server performance and error logs. This can provide the necessary data when upgrading servers and determining how much capacity is required. In IT, it's a bad idea to size systems too small. Over time, system and software updates slow down servers and desktops. Excess capacity is required, because you don't want to replace systems sooner than three years. However, after that time, warranties typically expire and system performance declines, so plan accordingly.

Motion: Create common sense policies to keep firefighting under control. Never update on a Friday, and never push the latest Windows updates and security patches to all computers. Stay one or two months behind, and have a series of test servers. A daily checklist should include monitoring various system logs for errors when preventative maintenance is performed.

Unused Employee Knowledge: Through the first 10 chapters of this book, there are several examples for how to motivate and involve people in the process. This is the real key that keeps the systems up and running. To retain the knowledge, systems are documented so that others can follow the standard procedures. Ticketing systems are used to report problems and resolutions. Automation tools are created and even scripted to reduce repetitive tasks, such as software installs and updates.

When communicating with other people, I also make the point of saying "we" instead of "I." It's a team effort of more than one person. People feel as though they are part of a team when you use the word "we" in meetings and one-on-one conversations.

Another aspect lean manufacturing talks about is batch size. Keep the batch size smaller, so if problems are detected, corrections can be made early on in the process and less waste will occur. How does that relate to IT? First, for a small business, there's no need for a dedicated help desk, because that simply adds more complexity and longer wait times to a resolution. For example, if a first-level support person struggles with a problem and decides that it's too complex, he or she has to send it onto a higher level.

My approach is more cross-functional and team-based. I train my staff to know how the business functions and what their role is within the business. No matter which IT person is involved, they try to fix users' problems. If they can't fix the problem, they know exactly who can. Also, when new solutions are being developed, they get an early draft or release to users and get them involved as soon as possible to make sure the proposed solution will solve their problem. If the solution doesn't work, they can adapt accordingly.

Knowledge allows for more flexibility. Really plug into your business, cross-train your staff, and shorten the feedback loop. A shorter feedback loop is equal to a smaller batch size—problems come to light faster, and then you can change directions if necessary. If a proposed project is not going as planned, you can quickly evaluate it and decide if changes need to be made so that you see positive results and a successful project. Plans can be modified to reflect your decisions and still keep the long-range goal intact.

The cloud is another method that can be used to implement lean IT. Cloud-based applications can be implemented in a shorter time frame than a traditional install. With the cloud, there's no need to install or set up the local infrastructure or maintain it over time. You can drastically reduce the amount of time it takes to evaluate several accounting packages if they are all cloud-based.

Apply Lean IT

The challenge of applying years of practice to lean IT is value stream mapping and figuring out how to modify the process to reduce the waste and make the operation more efficient.

Create and document processes for your SMB that follow the flow of the business and allow for flexibility. Try to identify and bring the problems to the surface so that they can be resolved. This is a difficult task for specialized manufacturing facilities that build custom tooling for each customer. Get involved in departmental meetings, and consider becoming an ISO 9000 auditor. This will help you learn other aspects of the business and adapt to the requirements.

When it comes to detecting problems, keep an open-door policy and listen to user complaints. Have checklists to monitor system status and error logs, and review them in IT staff meetings. Assign improvement tasks to IT staff so that they have responsibilities and authority to get things done.

Always question the way things run and if it makes sense for the business. For example, if the scheduler in the ERP system is never used, find out why. Are there problems with it? How do similar businesses use that application? Does the scheduler work for them? The purpose is to look for problems with the scheduler so that you can improve the use of it within the business. Handle the research in a professional manner, and treat all people involved in the process with respect and honesty to come up with a solution.

ITIL

Other lean IT initiatives can be extracted from Information Technology Infrastructure Library (ITIL), which is a set of practices for IT service management. However, I believe that ITIL is more suited to large organizations.

Over the years, I have used parts of ITIL to achieve a lean IT structure. I am not an expert in ITIL, but I think there are good components within it that are applicable to many businesses. For an SMB, not all of the ITIL is required, so take and use the parts that are appropriate and useful for your business.

Chapter 12

12 Know your business

Role of the Business

For IT to be successfully within a business, it's important to know the bigger picture. What's the role of the company? What service does the company provide to the customer? What are the future plans of the business? Are there going to be more services added in the future? This is where you need to network with key people in the business. Make your five-year plan based on the information that you gather.

For example, if your business wants to build a portal so that customers can gain access to shop floor scheduling to see the live progress of their job, this needs to be planned, because it's probably not something that can be done in a few minutes.

I also believe that senior management needs to be transparent. Don't pass along the information you think the people below you "require." Instead, pass along the raw information, and let people process it for themselves. Work together to understand how the information affects upper and lower management. Doing this engages the minds of the people lower in rank. Using an entire workforce to solve business issues is far better that just one person.

Departments

Each department has their own issues that they're dealing with. For optimal system performance, it's important to know the business processes and make sure they're understood by IT. Interdepartmental business continuity automation should be monitored to ensure functionality. From engineering to purchasing, some level of automation might occur when BOMs are generated, like the organization of outside service data to simplify the job of the purchaser. If the engineers miss a step, the process could fail, so have a check in place to monitor the engineers to make sure they're doing their job. IT can intervene if the process fails, and they can help the departments find a fix for the problem and prevent it from recurring in the future.

For example, within an ERP system (based on the systems that I'm familiar with), engineering needs to properly create items and add them to product structures so that 1) purchasing can buy them, 2) shipping can receive them, and 3) accounting can invoice for them. Follow up with each department to ensure business processes are being followed. Create and monitor operation reports that check the data structure and integrity within the system. Have quarterly meetings to follow up on the process. More than likely, you'll find issues with the process. Perhaps items are not getting priced correctly. These issues can be review with accounting, purchasing, and receiving to make sure everyone is following the process. It may be necessary to tweak the process to get the desired result.

In custom engineering environments, the variance is typically very high, which makes it difficult to have an ironclad process. Also, ERP systems have limitations. So, you need to find a process that works for the business and the ERP system it supports. Collaboration between the various departments is required to maintain and improve the system.

Consider this part of the continuous improvement process. Question and challenge the normal way of doing business with all departments. Gather all departments in a single meeting, discuss all of the issues, and allow every member to speak and present their concerns. More than likely, with all the departments present, new information will come to light, which will help the problem-solving process.

When our engineering, accounting, and purchasing representatives came together in this meeting, we learned that not all purchased items were put on BOMs for rebuild tooling. Shop floor personnel added some items, like hydraulic cylinders, during the disassembly process. However, when they weren't added by engineering to the BOM, they didn't get priced to the job. We decided that production had to be involved in the process to add the necessary requirements to the BOM.

Workflow

Understanding each department workflow is important. The heads of the department know their process, but they may not understand what happens in other departments. However, a decision to make the process easier in one department can make life extremely difficult for the next department.

Continuing the example above, a change made to how engineering structures a job in the ERP system may increase the purchasers' responsibilities. Say engineering decides they want to break up outside services by the job lot level to accurately capture costs. Well, on the purchasing side, they now have to generate a PO for each type of service per lot. If there are 20 pieces per lot, and five lots per job, that means the purchaser will have to do five times the data entry work to achieve the desired result.

This is why it's important to understand the workflow between departments and not make decisions for other departments without their involvement in the process. What seems trivial and logical without understanding the flow and impact to downstream processes can become a nightmare.

Pinch Points

There are critical things that can really break the business it they fail. From my experience, the main pinch points for a manufacturing SMB include network and storage, because they have local storage and high performance networks to service the engineering and NC programming workstations.

The network must always be available. If it fails, people can't work or share data, so there has to be a plan for recovery or repair—ideally within the hour. Core switches should always have dual power supplies, and there should always be one spare switch on the shelf.

If your core switches are over two years old, an identical replacement switch may no longer be available. I don't put service contracts on switches, because I find it more cost effective to buy a spare and have it available. Once it's used and goes into production, plan to have it replaced, get it configure, and test it out. If the same switch model is no longer available, do some research to find a compatible switch that will to the job, and then store it with the other spare parts.

This is a good example of why you should have identical spares. In a tight situation, the failed switch can be swapped out quickly with no compatibility issues. More time and effort can be put into finding a solution for the next time a switch fails. From past experience, I've found that network switches very rarely fail. I've had more issues with shop floor switches falling due to the condition under which they have to perform than switches located in the climate controlled IT room.

The next pinch point is the main storage server. In case of a major failure, have spares on hand and a recovery plan that's been tested. This goes hand in hand with the network. No network means no data, and no storage means no place to put the data. Have a recovery plan that you know works, and make sure someone's checklist includes the monitoring of network and storage equipment to keep everything running smoothly.

Specialty Apps

Only a few people typically use specialty applications, so it doesn't make sense to purchase and license them for every desktop. These applications can be layered in terminal servers and published so that some users get them, but not all. However, there will always be some applications that don't fit in properly and have special requirements.

For example, ADP Payroll was historically limited to run on Windows XP, and then it was grandfathered in with a dedicated VDI box. ADP is working on a new version that will be totally web-based. At the time of this writing, they are over-burdened with migrating users over to the new version. There must be a way to integrate odd-ball specialty applications into the network. The existing ADP application can run on a VDI computer and seamlessly integrate to a terminal services desktop so that anyone can access and run it.

Know the People

Along with getting to know the pinch points in a business, it's a good practice to know the people. Some people can't work if their computer is down. For example, you might have only one purchaser, and if he or she can't get into the ERP system to purchase things, this could affect production in an emergency situation.

Other people have tight deadlines, and unexpected tasks can be extremely stressful. So, be patient, and always do your best to help the people within the organization get their jobs done.

Industry Trends

Industry trends are important when managing IT operations for an SMB. Manufacturing is very different from other types of businesses—especially automotive tooling manufacturing, because it's affected by fluctuation in the economy. If the auto industry slows down, so do the manufacturers and suppliers. If the auto industry is building new models or revising power trains to meet EPA targets, then manufacturers and suppliers will be busier. This trend for IT is important, because it needs to fit within your plans to scale the business accordingly. It doesn't make sense to purchase and license expensive services if you know, at some point, they have to be scaled back. Senior management should have their finger on the pulse of the industry and communicate this information to all relevant departments.

This is not to say that you need to be cheap and do a sloppy job. Quite the contrary! When business is good, you need to upgrade and expand—like replacing old hardware and upgrading the ERP system. When the business slows down, ride out the low spots. It comes in cycles. I've seen it happen several times in manufacturing. Plan, be prepared, know your business, and work with senior management. Perhaps your business prefers to purchase equipment as opposed to leasing it. Communicate with the accounting department to understand how the purchasing process works.

This is also where the cloud can be a benefit or a hindrance, depending on the service you pick and how you use it. Take backups, for example. Say you purchase a bunch of licenses to backup several servers to a cloud provider, and this is the only way data is backed up. Well, you can't decide not to backup any servers, because you don't want to loose the data—that would be a hindrance. On the flip side, if you have a number of licenses for a software service that exists in the cloud, more than likely, if things slow down, some people may get laid off. These licenses could be removed from the cloud provider, thus saving some cash, which would be a huge benefit to the business.

So, when planning software purchases or cloud rollouts, take these things into consideration, and keep it simple and flexible. Do your research, and plan what is best for the business.

Grow with the Business

Once you become familiar with the business, you'll gain a better understand about how to operate. When times are good and things are booming—expand, replace, and upgrade. Your budget can be flexible from year to year. If you build the foundation and infrastructure correctly, as I've described in previous chapters, you won't be locked into long-term contracts or situations where you can't reduce your costs.

Have policies in place that evaluate software licenses, usage, and renewal on a yearly basis. If some software is not being used as much, it can be adjusted accordingly. This allows for flexibility within the business. Manufacturing goes through trends. When old projects require less engineering, drop these excess CAD software licenses.

Chapter 13

13 Service the Business

IT delivers a service to the business. It's important to understand the different operations of the business so that everything can be addressed in a logical, uniform way.

Operational Issues

In a small business, sufficient resources need to be allocated to deal with user issues and keep things under general repair. As I stated before, keeping production running is the first priority. It's important to always have sufficient resources available to handle operational issues in a timely fashion. Make sure IT staff know their roles, responsibilities, and priorities. Discuss these issues and business pinch points during weekly meetings. IT staff need feedback—good and bad—as to how they are doing with tasks. Point out issues and concerns, and the listen everyone's feedback, because it's important to get both sides of the story.

This is where I find a whiteboard useful. Have one available for IT so they can write down issues during the week that need to be discussed. Remember, this is an open forum where anyone can contribute. It's fairly common to have issues that drag on and affect production. Make sure you communicate these operational issues to the rest of the business.

For example, you could experience integration issues with older software running on newer PCs. One time, we had a Windows NT 4.0 application that was installed on Windows 7, but there were issues with file locking on the storage server and access to it wasn't stable. The storage server was based on Windows 2008 Storage Server. It took a few weeks to determine that a registry edit was required on the storage server and Windows clients for the application to work satisfactorily.

Luckily for us, there was a close relationship between IT and production, and resources were allocated to stay on this task until we found a resolution. This issue expanded several weeks, but it stayed on our whiteboard and was discussed at each meeting briefly until the task was complete. Ultimately, this was very important to the business and the shop floor, because it directly affected production.

Despite operational issues, everyone needs to take a vacation, even in a small business. When IT resources are tight, plan people's vacation time on the operational side so that staff can be moved around to sufficiently cover all operational issues. Make sure checklists are passed over as well, so all operational activities can be maintained.

New Tasks and Projects

Business-enhancing projects provide new functionality and offerings to increase productivity and automate previously long-winded complex processes. Operational issues are things that keep the business running as-is. The flip side to that is working on projects and systems that directly affect business productivity. In small manufacturing businesses, this is usually a big challenge. The operation side can be very complex, with many diverse applications, which can make it difficult to find the resources to put into business-enhancing products.

To keep the business running smoothly, you should have staff with very diverse skills, but that's not necessarily the best for working on dedicated projects. Having said that, generally speaking, people love challenges, and the best way to motivate people is provide a balance of new exciting projects with day-to-day routine work. I've always trained people to religiously use checklists, because they keep people on top of daily operations. So, split up the day. Allocate sufficient time in the morning to do routine tasks. Later in the day, schedule time for projects where a bigger chunk of time is required. I recommend using a calendar to plan your day.

Projects are a necessity to the business, just like operational issues. Know the priorities of the business, then train and organize your people effectively.

Managing the Business

After understanding that there's an operation side and a project side to the business that require attention, good project management and communication are required to keep everything running. As the department leader, you're always juggling tasks around—none of them ever stop, but the priorities shift with the requirements of the business. It's impossible with limited staff to work on all projects and have everything completed at the same time. Very few companies have unlimited resources, so you have to prioritize tasks and complete the most important ones first.

Again, this is where clear communication to other departments is required to keep everyone on the same page. Senior management needs to be aware and must support the efforts of the IT team.

The Need for Urgency

Based on my experience, I really don't see the point of people rushing around with their heads cut off, trying to urgently complete tasks. It's far better to paint the big picture, plan, allocate resources, and execute the task. Yes, there will be some surprises that you'll have to deal with. However, there will be a lot fewer mistakes if you take some time initially to get organized.

Have a plan for those times when urgency is required. Then delegate and provide the necessary resources, responsibility, and authority to the people who need to execute the plan.

In a truly lean and well-functioning organization, you'll have all the resources for your processes, so there should never be a situation that requires a need for urgency. Don't confuse this situation for an emergency or equipment failure. The need for urgency is a lack of communicating from senior management through the ranks.

Planning Ahead

I can't emphasize enough the importance of planning. Each department needs to plan and then communicate their objectives company-wide so that the necessary resources can be put in place.

One example of poor planning and lack of communication was a department that ordered a new piece of equipment that required network connectivity and access to the Internet. However, IT was notified the same day that the service guy came to configure the equipment. The person who ordered the equipment did not inform IT of the requirements. Since the location where the equipment was installed had no network ports anywhere nearby, the install couldn't be completed, and the service person was sent home. This is why it's important to know the business, get support from senior management, and communicate with various departments so that you can be made aware of what's coming down the pipe.

Within any organization, there needs to be some mechanism that shares out projects on-the-go internally, like a weekly or monthly newsletter. I will touch on some other tools that can be used to propagate this information in Chapter 20.

Subcontracting

Hiring subcontractors is sometimes key to delivering projects on time. The IT staff that keep the operation running are critical, but they are often stretched to handle too many projects that improve the business operational side. Subcontractors can be hired to come in and help. I typically use them for specific skills. For example, you shouldn't keep a web developer on staff if that only makes up 5% of the IT department. Find a skilled person, and subcontract the work to them. Doing this kind of work with in-house staff that are highly geared to keep things running doesn't make any sense.

The same thing applies to really tough technical issues. As I mentioned before, the staff that keeps the systems running are generalists. Most generalists have a well-rounded skillset and are problem solvers, but they know when they need help on a specific challenge. You'll find some people stronger at various tasks. Focus on their strengths, and use them accordingly. Hire subcontractors to crack the really tough technical issues and specific development tasks. The in-house IT staff can work and even manage the subcontractors where they overlap with tasks and projects.

Chapter 14

14 Purchasing

Redundant Servers and Network

Put your money into good quality hardware that does the job. All servers and core network switches should have redundant power supplies. "Best of breed" is not necessarily what you need. Remember that this is like the foundation of your house. If it's not built strong, it will collapse, and this is one area where you don't want headaches. Hardware failures usually happen at the most inconvenient time. I do my best to think about the primary servers and core switches to reduce the chances of hardware failure.

Planning and Communicating

Generally speaking, it's not a good idea to purchase something unless you've thought about it or planned for it. For example, when it's time to purchase some replacement network switches, write out a plan about what it is that you want to do, conduct some upfront research, and then send the request to your vendor.

If you have a good vendor, ask them to do some research as well. Then work together to come up with an optimum solution and price point. This helps the vendor to understand your environment and what you're looking for.

Don't buy the special of the week or day, especially if you don't need it. Don't set a budget initially. Instead, look for what will do the job, make your ultimate wish list, and see what it costs. Work with the vendor to fine-tune the quote. In the end, with your vendor's input, you'll have a well thought-out plan and a reasonable quote can be formulated. Vendors can come up with some very cost-effective and flexible solutions, but don't just blindly accept what they offer. You know the business and the requirements, so make a good choice. Treat the funds of the company as if they were your own.

Three Quotes

One of my policies is to use at least three vendors for purchases. Establish long-term relationships with your vendors. From time to time, especially with large purchases, do a price check between vendors. A new vendor may give a low price initially to get your business, but they'll jack up their price over time. It pays to shop around and know what things cost.

I believe in establishing long relations and good credit history with all the vendors I use. At some point in time, a crisis will arise. Maybe you'll experience a major failure in a server and, by chance, you won't have any spares. This is where having that long-standing vendor relationship can help.

Watch What You Buy

In situations where the newest hardware is not required, eBay is a good option. eBay often has replacements parts and/or offers fair prices for slightly older hardware, including Cisco routers and thin clients. However, if purchases are made on eBay, make sure that you're aware of the conditions of the purchase. Read the fine print so you know that you're getting what's being sold, not just what's in the picture. Do they have a return policy? Have they been in business a long time with a good track record? It's better to thoroughly investigate before you complete any transaction.

Good Quality

Stick with good, reliable products that have a proven track record. For example, if you purchase HP hardware, make sure replacement and spare parts are HP. Don't buy no-name products and hope that they'll work. If you're running a production environment, there's nothing more frustrating than installing new hardware components and having them fail premature or be dead on arrival (DOA).

Negotiate Contracts

Do your homework before purchasing. Ask questions and challenge the prices that you're given. If it's time to renew your ISP contract, get three quotes—and they don't need to be on the same media. Compare costs and functions between each to make sure they're offering the same features. The lowest cost is not necessarily the best. If your current vendor is offering good service, use the two other quotes as ammunition, and play them against one another until you get a price that meets the requirements of the business.

Purchasing Conclusions

Always remember, treat the company funds as if they are your own. When you buy a new computer for your home, don't you shop around and find the best price for what you require? Don't just listen to what the salesman says and buy anything on the spot.

Research, compare options and prices, and make the best choice that suits the needs of the business. Again, if it helps, use a decision matrix chart from the book *The Rational Manager.*

Chapter 15

15 Apps, Services, and Printers

Virtualization

Virtualization is nothing new, so if you're not using it, you better start. Don Dragomatz, a friend and former colleague, told me many years ago, "Find the trend, and ride the wave." You can use this philosophy as a general guide.

There's a lot of virtualization software available, like VMware, Microsoft Hyperv, and Zenserver, and they all have their strengths and weaknesses. If your shop is all Microsoft, then your best option might be to use Microsoft Hyperv, because it keeps the environment on one platform and simplifies troubleshooting. Plus, Microsoft skills and resources are plentiful. Hyperv has several nice built-in functions that aren't in the base ESXi server. For example, you can replicate active VMs to another Hyperv server. This is a good option to have. As VM hosts get upgraded, keep the old VM host server around as a standby backup for critical servers. For mail servers and ERP servers, it's a nice, simple way to have a backup server on standby for no additional cost.

VDI is also fully supported in the Microsoft environment with use of RemoteFX for high-end graphical workstations. This is supported right down to WYSE thin clients. Essentially, RemoteFX utilizes a graphics card in the server to accelerate graphic performance on the desktop, which is a thin client. It does this by a technique called screen scraping. The 3D codes are stripped off the remote session running on the server CPU and sent directly to the graphics GPU for processing. The end result is transmitted to the thin client for visual rendering.

VMware is very popular virtualization software, and it has some nice features that you won't find with Microsoft HyperV. On the same hardware platform, you'll achieve higher density with VMware than you will with Hyperv. If this is of greater importance than keeping everything Windows-based, then VMware is a better choice. Ultimately, do the necessary research to know your business and fulfill the requirements to keep it running.

Who Needs What?

How do you know who needs what? This is the most challenging task within the business. By utilizing the techniques that I've presented in these chapters, it is possible for you to understand the business and how it works. Then, when people within the company make requests, it should be apparent if they are valid or not.

For example, if a user comes to you and asks for a new license of some CAD software, more than likely, you'll say no. However, if you communicate with other parts of the business, you might learn about a contract for a job being quoted that requires new CAD software to design it. Believe me, you'll make your job much easier if you plug into the business and understanding how it works.

Printers

How many printers do you need? How do you name and manage them? Most users want a printer on their desk so that they don't have to walk across the room. However, it's not very cost effective to give everyone his or her own printer, because the cost to stock all the toner and keep them in repair can be quite expensive.

The best thing is to work with a vendor to remotely monitor the usage of each printer and automate the inventory of toner. Purchase as many identical printers as possible if users absolutely need them located in their office. Have centrally located all-in-one printers for busier office areas. Working with a vendor for cost analysis is very beneficially, plus it helps suit the needs of the users. For example, shared office printers can be configured to securely print confidential documents. Most newer printers allow user accounts to save print jobs to memory. Thus, your print job will not be seen on the public shared printer until you desire it to be printed. Simply walk up to the printer, identify yourself (login), and your document will print safely and securely.

Purchasing may require a dedicated printer, but you can possibly reduce that by electronically printing POs and emailing directly from the ERP system. With a little work, you can modify the business processes to reduce printing and the number of printers. For the printers that you do keep, create a naming standard, document it, and share that information with the company on an internal web page.

Internal Web Server

Internal web servers are great for communicating standards and documents to users. Some common things to publish include phone extensions list, printer names and locations, and simple how-to documents. Honestly, you should communicate all the information within the business that helps users do their jobs.

From within Active Directory, set the default home page for all web browsers to the internal web page. So, when new things are published or changes are made, the end user is informed.

IT Change Management

Change management is the controlled identification and implementation of required changes to a computer system. It can be an internally or externally hosted system that tracks IT system changes. Before any change is made, capture the current state, document, and plan the desired state. Next, make the change, document the steps, and provide your reasoning. This is a good practice to follow so that it can be undone or restored to a previous working state if a problem arises after the change is performed.

Documentation is also good for historical purposes and recurring problems. You don't require fancy, expensive software for change management as long as the process is done thoroughly, well managed, and doesn't take excessive time to use. Keep it simple and useful. This is important to be able to prosper and grow as a business.

ERP to PLM

ERP and PLM systems have been around for many years, and they are increasingly maturing. There are many things an ERP system can do today that could replace a PLM system. However, I believe they are unique enough processes to be kept as separate, but tightly integrated, systems.

A PLM system's strength is being able to tightly hook into and manage engineering data. It has an inherent understanding of the product structure, material type, dimensions, and components. An ERP's strength is the execution of the process, which includes purchasing, receiving, and manufacturing.

Careful thought, study, and planning are necessary to segregate the roles into the correct systems. ERP/PLM require you to know and understand how the business functions. The planning and implementing of these types of systems is beyond the scope of this book. However, if they exist within your environment, they must be included as operational systems, and they need to be managed and kept up to date. Integrate the required processes for these systems, such as backups and updates, into the operation side of your IT plans.

Chapter 16

16 Application Delivery

Application delivery helps keep your environment easy and simple to manage, so don't overcomplicate it. Use the tools you have, including the tools that are built into Windows, to your advantage. However, be cautious, because some tools will add work to your team without providing business benefits or automation.

Layering

Layering is a concept that I find very beneficial. Instead of installing ERP clients on every computer, simply publish them through terminal services. Installs and updates are performed on one server, in one location. Installs are scripted and automated, then pushed out to computers and other terminal servers. When the user logs into their primary desktop and launches the ERP application, it runs on a dedicated terminal server. This speeds up the installs and greatly simplifies troubleshooting.

Terminal Servers and Thin Clients

Setting up thin clients is a simple process, but there's a fair bit of upfront planning and structuring work that needs to take place to have them work effectively as a direct desktop replacement. To determine whether thin clients are suitable for your organization, begin with a list of users in each department. Compile a list of all the applications these people use, and eliminate as many redundant applications as possible. For example, if you have five applications that do the same thing, like editing pictures, pare the list down to one. Do this by gathering user feedback and involving them in the process. Make sure all the applications are terminal services friendly, and then test them on a terminal server to see if they all work together. Ultimately, the fewer the applications, the faster and more stable the server is and the easier it is to maintain.

From past experience, I've found that WYSE makes some very nice zero management thin clients based on their ThinOS. They boot up, look for a DHCP server, get an IP address and TFTP server, then download and use their own configuration file. Doing this makes it easy to centrally setup and manage all the thin clients.

Once the thin client is selected, set up and test the environment to make sure everything works as expected before going live. Based on the feedback from testing, modifications can be made and retested until a satisfactory system can be built to replace traditional desktop PCs. Test with the people who will be using the system, because they need to perform equal or better than a standalone desktop to be successful.

Also, make sure you adhere to Microsoft licensing. For Terminal Services, a TS CAL and a Server CAL are required for each desktop user accessing the terminal server.

VDI vs. Terminal Services

What is the difference between VDI and Terminal Services, and when do you use one over the other? VDI is basically a virtually hosted desktop computer that is totally isolated from any other hosted service. If a VDI computer crashes, it doesn't affect any other users. A terminal server is one large server that hosts a desktop for many users. If one user badly crashes, it can possibly affect other users, and there's also a small chance that it will crash the server.

In a situation where there are many lightweight users that use all similar applications, such as accounting and purchasing, using a terminal server will help keep management highly centralized and add the most bang for the buck, so to speak.

Power users that use higher end, compute-intensive CAD applications may require VDI computers. This provides the best performance for the end user but also adds a level of management. It's still much better than a desktop PC, because there isn't a hardware aspect that needs to be serviced or maintained.

One-Off Applications

Only a few people require access to one-off applications, so don't keep them on a terminal server. The majority of users who do general office work—accounting, purchasing, production, shipping, receiving, and reception—all could have a standard terminal server desktop. If accounting and shipping need access to some specific one-off applications, they can be delivered on a separate terminal server. If these applications are not compatible with a terminal server, you can deliver them through a dedicated VDI computer.

Another thing that I've done in the past is keep a few shareable multimedia computers located in various parts of the company. These are full workstations that support a wide range of needs, and it provides some flexibility to people who require it.

Remote Access

In this day and age, people are plugged in all the time. Users on the road, at home, and in remote offices may need access to their full desktop. A lot of problems can be quickly solved with access to corporate system, which makes remote access increasingly important.

Centralizing your data, management, and control gives you the ability to have anyone acquire access to their desktop at any place, as long as they have a connection to the Internet. I've been using these tools since Windows NT 4.0. They've come a long way and are now quite robust.

All Windows desktop computers come with a remote desktop application that allows easy access to their office desktop. A simple SFTP site can be set up so that users can download and run preconfigured RDP files. I recommend using a terminal server gateway, because it's a simple and secure method to publish and share out desktops.

A terminal services gateway can be used to eliminate the need to support VPNs for regular desktop users. I find this greatly simplifies the end users' task of connecting to their corporate desktop. There's no need for a VPN to be established, because the configuration is performed within the remote desktop application that's built into Windows to provide a secure connection.

The added benefit here is that terminal servers and VDI computers can exist anywhere—the corporate head office, remote office, or even the cloud. This is the architecture of the future.

Mobile Access

Paving the way from remote access leads directly into mobile access. There are several RDP clients that support a terminal server gateway for iPhone and Android devices. Unfortunately, there are not many for BlackBerry. Windows operating systems have a built-in RDP client, which support things like a terminal services gateway.

Work with your mobile device management (MDM) provider so that you can get remote access to any web-based reports or applications. You want to create a simple centrally managed environment that's based on common tools, and then extend that to remote access and mobile access that leads up to the cloud.

Chapter 17

17 Special Projects

What Are Special Projects?

I classify a "special project" as something like a new ERP system implementation. It isn't something that's done day-to-day, and the skill set may not exist within the company. When done correctly, these projects can greatly increase the productivity of the business.

This does not mean that another person needs to be hired full-time to the IT department. You must plan and determine if more resources are required temporarily, or perhaps it would make more business sense to hire a subcontractor.

Discuss special projects with senior management so that they understand the current capacity of the IT department and if they're able to do the project or require further assistance.

Benefits to the Company

The outcome of special projects needs to show how they will improve the overall functionality of the business.

A good example is the selection and implementation process of new CAM programming software. The old software had been in use for about 15 years, with no major functional improvements for many years. The license for the software was very costly. A business plan was put together to investigate new software. The plan detailed how each software package would be tested in-house on real jobs. This was a major purchase, and the only way to properly validate the NC programming software was to use it and see how it worked. An existing NC programmer was brought on board and trained to use the software, and real production jobs were made to evaluate the software performance.

The original plan laid out specific things that had to be improved. For example, there needed to be three times reduction in NC programming, enhanced abilities to control tool paths, and greater automation of repeatable tasks. The goal was to dramatically increase the production in the CAM department without an increase in staff.

Who Do You Involve in Special Projects?

Let's continue with our example from above. Several departments had to be involved in this special project. The NC programming department was impacted the most. One NC programmer was selected to test the software and work with the resellers. Testing was performed in the NC programming office so that all members of the department could get involved and see the results for themselves.

During the testing phase, various shop floor machine operators were involved, because their feedback was required to compare the quality of the output from the old software to the new.

The engineering department was also involved, since output from this department flows to the NC programming department. Basically, engineering designs the parts and NC programming has to machine them. Since data is imported to the new CAM system, and data compatibility is important, engineering input was essential.

It's important to know the business and how information flows through the company. Who are the downstream and upstream customers? This is the best way to select the people who need to be directly involved, because they are the key stakeholders. Identify these people early on in the process, and make sure upper management is involved. These people also have the responsibility to help communicate project progress through their respective department.

The purpose is to get everyone involved in the process (get buy in) so they can have their say. It can be a positive project that shows the business is concerned about the future and increasing productivity if everyone feels like they are part of it. This is a motivational project that will keep the business on the leading edge of technology.

How Do You Manage Special Projects?

Depending on the scope of the project, various tools are available. The NC programming software selection project was a large-scale project that touched multiple departments. A project of this scale required project management software like Microsoft Project, a project manager, and one dedicated full-time job for an NC programmer.

Big projects must be reviewed with the affected department heads and senior management. It is critical that senior management provide full support and grant the necessary authority and responsibility to the leader of the project.

Change is sometimes difficult but necessary. Even though affected departments have been involved in the process and are kept aware of what's happening, there are always some people who resist change. Be patient, hear people out, and work with them to overcome their concerns and learn to accept the new process.

Your testing results need to show documented proof that the new process will grant desired results. The people closest to the project should also have a gut feeling that it's the right thing to do.

Schedule regular meetings to review the project with key stakeholders. The meetings could be by weekly or monthly, depending on the project. Prepare agendas for each meeting and keep them running on time. Make sure each member of the meeting has an opportunity to give his or her input. Document the results of the meeting and send out minutes that include action items, people responsible, and key deadlines. The next meeting should begin with a review of the action items from the previous meeting. Finally, keep a running tab of the meeting agendas for historical purposes.

People Change Management

This is similar to IT change management, but it affects the people and is a very important piece to the whole process. People need to be involved and feel as though they are part of the process. Do your best to be transparent and communicate the reason why the change is required. Provide examples of how it will improve the business overall.

People will not change for the sake of change. They need to believe that the change is of benefit to them and their job.

Tools to Manage

Before the project begins, write out the project plan. What steps and approximate timing are required for this project? Outline your resources and funds. I use tools that provide a good high-level overview of the project, with milestones and deliveries, so that I can track sub-projects and tasks that wrap up into a larger project. Sometimes, I use Windows Excel, because it's simple and can be altered to suit many different project types. Also, being a Mac user, I've created custom templates in Bento to manage large-scale projects, because it syncs with your calendar for tasks and reminders.

To get a high-level overview of the project and timelines, the task data can easily be imported into Microsoft Project and viewed in Gantt format. This is great for meetings, so everyone can visually gauge the overall status of a project. However, I personally think that Microsoft Project requires too much time, unless that's your full time job or a large scale project. When I'm working with a project, I prefer tools that are fast and easy to use and update.

How to Subcontract

Some projects require subcontract work, where a part of the project is developed outside of the company because there aren't sufficient resources in-house to perform the required task. Write a very detailed software specification for quoting purposes. I believe in using rapid development techniques. Leverage the technical abilities of good developers to keep the design simple and cost effective. You should also use the knowledge of the end users to create a simple but usable end product.

Document your discussions and any key decisions that are made. Make sure that responsible people are identified and that they clearly understand the project requirements. Establish clear delivery dates, and then follow up to make sure everyone is on task.

Chapter 18

18 Management

Over time, I've learned that company culture is very important for a business to be successful. Treat people fair, be open, and remain honest. People are not machines—they run your processes and ultimately make your business.

Motivation and Leadership

Leadership is not micromanaging or ordering people how to do things. Rather, it's about building an environment where people can flourish. State the vision and guide people along its path. Motivate people to do better and improve. Involve people in the process to take ownership. Teaching, guiding, and mentoring are all part of leadership.

I believe that leadership is for people and about people. Good values, manners, morals, ethics, principles, and beliefs create a strong foundation to lead effectively, authentically, honestly, and with integrity.

Here is a summarized list of what a leader's duties should include:

- Unleash peoples' passion

- Engage peoples' creativity

- Get people involved, give them a voice

- Challenge peoples' intellect

- Get people to care

- Recognize peoples' contributions

- Keep your commitments

- Give responsibility and authority

Know Your People

As I mentioned in previous chapters regarding different personality types, if you're the IT leader, you need to be aware that not all people are created equally, nor do they respond the same by using the same methods of communication.

For example, if you know that one of your staff members is an introvert, you can tailor your communication and position that person toward tasks that use their abilities and talents. Introverts don't like being put in the spotlight, so give them information they need in advance to study and prepare for meetings. Quite often, they'll come to the meetings with some very unique perspectives. This provides a comfortable working space for that person and allows them to thrive.

If one of your staff is an extrovert, that person is more likely to voice his or her opinion in meetings. Extroverts typically are very comfortable in the spotlight. So, provide challenges that allow the extroverts on your team to excel.

Upper Management

Many upper management positions are staffed with extroverts. This is a fundamental problem, because many extroverts don't grasp the big picture or communicate it. In positions of power, extroverts tend to micromanage, not delegate tasks and take responsibility for other peoples' work.

This is a clear recipe for disaster in any organization that doesn't value people. Processes don't run themselves, people do. It's the responsibility of upper management to communicate the goals of company and how it services the customer. If the big picture is communicated to all the business leaders with a clear direction of where the company is going, it becomes much easier to align the processes within the business to meet those goals.

Management fails where it hoards the information and tries to tightly control the business. Everyone has a job to do. The VP of the company is in no position to tell an IT person or a shop floor person how to do his or her job. However, a VP should have a sense of what people are doing and constantly communicate the big picture to each business unit about how they fit into the overall plan. I can't say enough how important this is. Everyone within the organization needs to feel as though they are included and doing their job to better the business.

Clear, honest communication is required between senior management and the business or department leaders. This is vital to the health of your organization. Business leaders also need to listen to their departments and communicate effectively. They must understand how their business functions and then communicate that to all corners of the business. Don't get mixed up with politics along the way.

A final comment on leadership is this quote from Bob Lutz, the former vice president of General Motors, in his book *Car Guys vs. Bean Counters*:

"It applies in any business. Shoemakers should be run by shoe guys, and software firms by software guys, and supermarkets by supermarket guys. With the advice and support of their bean counters, absolutely, but with the final word going to those who live and breathe the customer experience. Passion and drive for excellence will win over the computer-like, dispassionate, analysis-driven philosophy every time."

This is common sense for any business leader. Use your product people to improve your products and help your business grow.

Chapter 19

19 Security

Security is an important part of every business, but it's sometimes overlooked. There's a fine line between securing things too much and hampering the business.

Big Bad IT

It is key that you have the support of senior management and that they understand the importance of security. The IT department aren't control mongers—they're simply looking out for the best interest of the business. The prime directive is to keep productions systems up and running, safely and securely at a reasonable cost. What does it take to do this? If you've followed the chapters in this book, you'll be very plugged into the business and know the requirements.

Work with all the departments so that they understand the need for security. Create a security policy that's appropriate for the business, and then train the IT department so that they can enforce it. However, remain open at all times to receive feedback about the policy.

Part of the IT department's job is to identify what to secure and how to secure it. It must also determine the acceptable risks to the business.

Keep Security Simple

When you make security overly complex, it can complicate your infrastructure and cost additional resources to maintain it. A firewall is only securing the endpoint of your network—who and what is allowed access to and from the Internet. Physical and device security also needs to be considered, as well as acceptable use of corporate equipment.

Create a network acceptable use policy that's suitable for your business, and then circulate it to all employees and new hires. This should be part of a package that's distributed to new employees. Have the document signed by each employee to verify that they've been informed of the policy.

Here is a sample network policy:

Corporate Internet and Network Systems.

OWNER / AUTHOR:

ENVIRONMENT / CLASS:

IMPACTED ENTITIES:

REFERENCES:

DESCRIPTION:
Describes the Internet and Network policies in place

CAUTIONARY NOTES:

COMMENTS:

BODY:

Company name corporately provides and maintains a link to the Internet for their IT systems, workstations, mobile, tablets, and servers. The corporate link to the Internet, remote network links (VPN) to other corporations, and remote access facilities are regarded by *company name* as corporate services and assets. *Company name* endeavors to protect these corporate assets and services by applying a corporate policy as assumed and/or explicitly stated. All Internet and all remote network assets/services as provided by *Company name* to its employees and affiliates (Authorized Users) will be governed by the General Use Guideline and Acceptable Corporate Use Policy.

Acceptable Corporate Use Policy

The *Company name* Internet Link and Network Resources (remote access systems) provide the facilities for professional corporate communications. These facilities include the provision of email, and network services (file transfer, web browsing, and hosting,) inside and outside the corporation.

⇒ These facilities are to be used in a professional manner for communication regarding *Company name* business.

⇒ As part of the support of these facilities, *Company name* will monitor the use of these facilities.

⇒ Monitoring the use of the facilities is a standard maintenance process at *company name.*

⇒ The maintenance procedures may or may not require detailed examination/evaluation of communications protocols and, as an example, expose the contents of specific email as well as other communications utilities provided on the corporate network.

⇒ *Company name* reserves the right to examine all communications as provided by the services in the corporate network. Users are specifically advised they have **no privacy.**

⇒ If detailed examination/analysis of corporate communications reveals breaches in Policy, *Company Name* may take appropriate action.

Acceptable Corporate Use Policy

1. Use can be:
   1.1. Communication and exchange for professional development, to remain professionally current or debate issues in a field of knowledge;
   1.2 For professional activities or work related professional associations and research development;
2 Passwords:
   1. It is recommended that passwords are changed every 6 months.
   2. Passwords should be pass phrases, not birthdays or names.
   3. Passwords should be greater that 15 characters in length.
2. Screen locking:
   2.1. Computer screens must be locked when the user is not at his/her desk.
3. Software requirements/licensing:
   3.1. Users will contact *responsible person/ department* if new software is required.
   3.2. If new software is to be downloaded and install on company computers, users must contact the *responsible person/ department*.
   3.3. All software used on company property must be legally licensed.

Unacceptable Corporate Use Policy

1. The *Company name* Corporate Link and Network may not be used for any of the following:
    1. The creation or transmission of any offensive, obscene, or indecent images, data, or other material, or any data capable of being resolved into obscene or indecent images or material;
    2. The creation or transmission of material that is designed or likely to cause annoyance, inconvenience, or needless anxiety;
    3. The creation or transmission of defamatory material;
    4. The transmission and storage of material that infringes the copyright of another person or corporation, including music, video, and literary products in any format;
    5. The excessive storage of personal data, including music, pictures, or video files.
    6. The transmission of unsolicited commercial or advertising material either to other Organizations, except where that material is embedded within, or is otherwise part of a service to which the member of the Organization has chosen to subscribe;

(ex. sending or storing an email with an attached joke)

7. Deliberate unauthorized access to facilities or services accessible via the Internet; (ex. accessing a private file transfer site without that Organization's consent)

8. Use of the computer or Internet services for personal use during work hours, unless authorized by your supervisor.

9. Deliberate activities with any of the following characteristics:

    1. Wasting staff efforts or networked resources, including time on end systems accessible via the Internet and the effort of staff involved in the support of those systems

    2. Corrupting or destroying other users' data;

    3. Violating the privacy of other users;

    4. Disrupting the work of other users;

    5. Using the Internet in a way that denies service to other users (ex. deliberate or reckless overloading of access links or of switching equipment);

    6. Continuing to use an item of networking software or hardware

after *Company name* has
requested that use cease because it
is causing disruption to the correct
functioning of *Company name*
Network, including the Internet
link;

7.   Other misuse of the Internet or
networked resources, such as the
introduction of viruses;

2.   Where *Company name* Network or Internet Link
is being used to access another network, any
abuse of the acceptable use policy of that
network will be regarded as unacceptable use of
the *Company name* Network (ex. If someone
accesses another network and does not follow the
policy of that network)

3.   Users are not permitted to download, install, or
run any executable program without consent
from *responsible person/department*. This
includes installing software from a CD-ROM or
Internet download. All software within
Company name must abide by the corporate
policies.

4.   Users will not share their password with any
other *Company name* Employee.

5.   Never use the "save password" option on any
application, Internet, or form.

Confidentiality

1   Customer data must be kept confidential, secure, and stored in a non-public location with limited access to authorized personal only.
     1.   Any document containing sensitive pricing information such as quotes.
     2.   Any files containing Customer information or *Company name* privileged information. (pictures, projects, or PowerPoint)

Acknowledgement of Understanding

I have read and agree to comply with the terms of this policy governing the use of the computer network at *Company name*. I understand that violation of this policy may result in disciplinary action, including possible termination and civil and criminal penalties.

Printed Name:

_____

Signature:

_____

Date:

_____

Have a policy for mobile devices, including personally owned devices that access the corporate network. Set a standard for what's acceptable for securing the environment. MDM software is also available at a reasonable cost, like Air Watch and Mobile Iron. Perhaps you just need a way to make sure no devices are rooted or jailbroken and to provide secure access to corporate documents. Do some research and figure out what will work best for your business.

Here is a sample mobile policy:

Smartphones Policy

Date

Supported Devices

Currently supported smartphones for connecting to *Company name*, Exchange for email, and calendaring functions:

Smartphone - Operating System Requirements	Software Security
1) *model A*	*Description A*
2) *model B*	*Description B*

Currently, we do not support any other smartphone or tablet devices.

Security Concerns

Smartphones and tablets are amazing tools for increasing productivity. However, they have some security issues that you need to be aware of. Jailbreaking or rooting is a process that installs a modified operating system onto the device so that you can download non-signed applications. The downside of jailbreaking is that the operating systems and applications run without a software verification process to screen for potentially malicious code. The verification process itself may not be 100% perfect, but it is the first line of defense. All applications run as the root user account, which has full access to anything on the device. Essentially, it circumvents any security on the device.

There is a highest risk on Android-based phones of installation applications with some sort of malicious code. It is imperative that users only install applications from Google's Play Store on their Android device. Also, the device must not be rooted—only the original OEM OS should be installed.

Malicious Code

Malicious code is a term used to describe an application that has been designed to cause undesirable affects, security breaches, or damage to a system (viruses and malware).

What Will Be Done

To ensure the reliability and security on our mail server and corporate network, the following will be implemented:

1. *Company name* will no longer support any device that does not meet the above stated criteria - nor will it be allowed access to the *Company name* network.
2. Regular audits to guarantee your phone meets the above requirements and ensure the security of *Company name* network.
3. Alternatively to the regular audits, the user of the device can allow the *Company name* to manage the device with *X MDM software.*

Smartphones are considered personal devices, and it is understood that there can be personal and sensitive information on them. The goal here is to ensure that they are secure, while minimizing the chance of damage to *Company name* corporate network.

By allowing your device to connect to *Company name* email server, you are agreeing to let *Company name* manage the security of your device, including but not limited to: disable access to the SD card, disable and remotely wipe the device if reported lost or stolen, and disallow remote desktop access to other devices.

Acknowledgement of Understanding

I have read and agree to comply with the terms of this policy governing the use of smart devices on *Company name* network. I understand that violation of this policy may result in disciplinary action, including possible termination and civil and criminal penalties.

Printed Name:

_____

Signature: _____

Date: _____

What to Secure?

Corporate data stored on your files servers needs to be secured, and all the data generated by various parts of the business must be securely filed. People should only have access to the data they need to do their jobs. For example, you don't want shop floor staff having access to sales or financial data. Know your business, find out who needs access to what data, and secure the information appropriately. Once you understand how your business works, setting up secure storage is an easy process.

Physical security, like access to the IT room, must be controlled and monitored. The IT room door should be locked at all times, and only authorized personal should have access. Document your software media and spare parts, and then store them in a safe location under lock and key that's only accessible by authorized personal.

Keep it simple when it comes to customer access to the Internet. I recommend having a separate Wi-Fi network for external customers and internal users. Keep all smartphones and tablets on the open Wi-Fi network. Allow secure access through the firewall to secured services. This is the simplest way to keep data secure. However, be cautious of rooted or jailbroken devices. If they're compromised, they could infect your network. There's nothing wrong with having multiple networks as long as they are managed simply and make sense. Research, plan, implement, and document what is right for your business.

Passwords

These days, I have way too many passwords to manage—one for each bank account, my home ISP, each email account, payroll, expenses, CRA, and the list goes on. The last thing you want to see is people sticking post-it notes around their desks with login and password information. Try to have a simple sign-on integrated to Active Directory wherever possible to reduce user headaches. The actual passwords don't need to be complex numbers, letters, and characters. That only enforces the need for people to write them down on post-it notes.

I think passphrases are a much better option. Keep the length to a minimum of 15 characters. For example, a phrase like *myd0ghasbige8rs* is "my dog has big ears," but I substituted the letter "o" for a zero and the letter "a" for the number eight. Everything is one word and lowercase. This keeps the password much easier to remember, and with sufficient length, an automated program trying to crack the password will take longer than a short cryptic password with fewer characters.

Why is Security Important?

Security protects your company's assets from risks. What are acceptable risks to your business? Does it make sense to give everyone access to all the data? Does everyone in the company need access to payroll information? Does everyone in the company need

Internet access? Do shop floor personnel require access to customer data? Does the customer have any security information in their contract that prohibits the sharing of their data? As the head of IT, it's your responsibility to answer these questions. If you don't have these answers, you need to get to know your business better.

Data must be protected from people outside the company who want to hack into your network to acquire your corporate knowledge. You also need to protect your data from people inside the company. Secrets can be sold to competitors by disgruntle employees. In fact, statistics show that you are as much at risk from internal staff as you are from external threats.

Denise Deveau wrote an article in the *Financial Post* called "Data theft as much an internal threat as it is external" (http://business.financialpost.com/executive/risk-management/data-theft-as-much-an-internal-threat-as-it-is-external). Here are some bullet points from her article:

• 50% of employees who left or lost their jobs kept confidential information, and 40% planned to use it in their new jobs

• Often employees believe they are the rightful owners of data, since they played a part in creating it or contributing to it

- You have to be very careful who you give access to what and monitor your Internet to make sure stuff is not going out the door

- Many employees have their own Dropbox accounts and send copies of their documents to Dropbox for access at home

- Even though encryption is beatable, it takes a lot of time, money, and computer hours to crack if it's done well

- Most cloud providers are far more secure than the average organization. They should be putting more time and effort into basic security things, like web applications, firewalls, monitoring, and segmenting their networks

Chapter 20

20 Future thoughts

The Cloud

The direction of technology is clear, so find the trend and ride the wave. Know your business and apply common sense to get the desired results. If it's not clear now, it will be soon. Technology is headed towards the cloud. There are countless businesses and several services that are now only offered through the cloud. For financial businesses, the entire operation could more easily be built in the cloud than a manufacturing business.

Following the advice that I've offered in these chapters, you can design your internal systems with layers and keep them simple so that parts (or all) can be moved into the cloud when the time is right. Document your systems and processes so that you can keep track of them when they eventually do move to the cloud.

There are a few more services that can be added to help. For example, Okta or OneLogin allow cloud services to be more easily integrated into your existing environment. This is a better choice than trying to get

Microsoft's Active Directory Federation Services to work.

There are a lot of resources on the Internet where you can learn about how to fit the cloud into your organization. Toronto Cloud Business Coalition (http://www.businesscloud.to) is a group that's leading the way with cloud adoption. TCBC has boot camps and workshops geared towards helping your business move to the cloud.

Also with cloud computing, economics of scale come into play. When you install a hypervisor in your business, you'll probably use only 80 to 90% of the capacity and have perhaps 15 to 20 servers per hypervisor. In the cloud, the host provider would have thousands of customers, potentially hundreds of servers per hypervisor, and probably utilize nearly 100% of the capacity of the server. More than likely, they'll have more fault tolerant and secure servers. This allows the provider to run a much more cost-effective setup. Instead of you purchasing new hardware every three years, you spend a monthly fee and rent the required servers in the cloud. The provider will be responsible for maintaining the infrastructure, and you just use the hardware and storage services. This makes it much easier and faster for you to roll out new servers and services.

Beyond Virtualization

Virtualization is here to stay, so you should virtualize as much of your environment as possible. Next to virtualization are containers, which is like virtualization of virtualization. This technology has been around for some time. However, it's maturing, and more usable products will coming out of this technology.

For example, Docker is an open-source project that automates the deployment of applications inside software containers. It provides an additional layer of abstraction and automation of operating system-level virtualization on Linux, Mac OS, and Windows.

License servers are ideally suited for these kinds of containers. One day, perhaps containers can be used to reduce licensed server complications.

VDI as a Service

VDI as a service is hosted in the Internet desktop, where the customer pays a monthly fee for the use of the service. Hence, the customer does have to bother with the desktop infrastructure.

At some point in the near future, I truly believe that desktop workstation computers will become obsolete. All desktops will become virtual, and a thin client or tablet-based computer will be used to access the desktop. The technology has been around for many years to do this, but it's only now becoming cost justifiable to implement. The applications and licensing process are lagging behind and will be the final pieces to really allow VDI as a service to take over for SMB manufacturers using complex engineering software.

There are several applications that are not fully designed to take advantage of a virtualized platform, nor are they design to be centrally installed. This is a must for virtualization to succeed.

Application licensing structures need to mature for this to evolve and take off. However, I am certain that it's only a matter of time before this becomes a reality.

Internet of Things

The Internet of Things (IoT) is the network of physical objects or "things" embedded in electronics, software, and sensors that are connected and exchange data with one another or a central database. IoT technology will radically change businesses processes. The example I provide in this section describes how IoT can be used to automate, integrate, and simplify manual processes. However, my particular example is geared towards manufacturers of large complex components that are custom designed and built, not those of mass assembly. Tools are readily available for this type of manufacturing.

Within a tooling manufacturing facility, raw material or steel is purchased. This material can be retrofitted with a magnetic radio frequency identification (RFID) tag that acts as a unique electronic serial number for this piece throughout the entire manufacturing lifecycle.

The entire manufacturing facility is outfitted with readers, and they're strategically placed to divide the building into zones, departments, or cells. So, as the piece moves throughout the building, its location is always known. For example, when the piece moves to a machine in waiting area, it could be tagged and registered as waiting on machine XYZ. This data can further be used to instantly determine the number of pieces in wait mode. Information like this is crucial for lean manufacturing practitioners to improve the operation of their business.

A machining center could also be outfitted with a reader. The RFID tag would need to be removed from the work piece and placed on the machine in a designated location. The reader would automatically clock time on the machine for this particular piece, and that information could be fed into a central database, like an ERP system. When manufacturing machines are directly connected to the network, information from the machine can be automatically captured. Again, the more detailed information that is gathered, the more intelligent decisions can be made.

Employees could use RFID tags for attendance by clocking onto a job. RFID sensors could be located at doorways so that employees' entrance is automatically recorded. Employee time on a particular machine can also be recorded and clocked against the job in the ERP system.

Doing this could completely automate the manual processes of clocking time against jobs and reduce the errors that go with it. Also, if pieces get transferred between jobs, you can easily reallocate the hours, because they are attached to the RFID tag or electronic bar code. All of this data is centrally collected. Dashboards can be built to display the status of jobs within the building.

If any outside service on production pieces are required, the magnetic RFID tag could be removed from the piece and placed in a zone that indicates the piece is no longer in the building. So, at any point in time, it's possible to know exactly where pieces are, their percentage of completion, and the cost of the job. This is done with minimal human intervention, which eliminates countess errors.

IoT technology is here today, but it's underutilized in many small custom-order manufacturing businesses. We already know that scheduling systems don't work as effectively as they could. Now that it's possible to know where everything is, a pull system could be development that identifies and prioritizes urgent jobs. Massive amounts of data could be captured, analyzed, and used for business improvement.

Data Centers

Software design data centers are already here. However, the tools that manage them and the building blocks that are used to build them need to grow and improve. Today, bare metal servers with massive SAN data warehouses are built. They are powerful and complex systems, and specific, costly skill sets are required to build and maintain them.

I believe this also needs to mature to an approach more like what Nutanix is doing. Their approach is modular and allows them to scale and ramp up easily and quickly, so that they're not hindered by the time it takes to build a complex traditional data center virtualization platform.

In a small business, it may not be financially justifiable to take such an approach. However, it is possible to study this technology and figure out where it fits within your business. It would be nice to be able to use standard building blocks to simplify and standardize the infrastructure and allow easy and limitless growth.

Manufacturing

For machining centers, the newer generations of controls are highly advanced and tightly connected to your internal network. There is a lot more information being collected within the machine control. It's now much easier to get uptime, spindle speed, feed, and cutter load remotely. Combining this information with the IoT, a business can compile massive amounts of data about its business.

For example, you can notify operators automatically that service is required or oil needs to be changed. You can even contact the machine reseller and commit diagnostic information directly to them. Then you can use that information as feedback into your NC programming software to build NC programs specific for each machining center to enhance the overall cutting process and reduce the total machining time.

One system that's currently available is Pulse by Lemoine Technologies. Its purpose is to monitor and collect data from the shop floor and present dashboards for machine utilization. The integration of something like Pulse will be much easier with newer intelligent machine controls.

This is the beginning of establishing what is called Big Data on a small scale for SMB manufacturers. Once the collection of data has begun, it can be studied in detail and examined for trends. For example, if the goal is to keep machines running within certain tolerance specifications, by gather and monitoring machine data, maintenance can be contacted and scheduled to optimize performance.

As a piece moves through a manufacturing facility, its electronic bar code includes inspection data, which ties it back to various equipment. By monitoring the accuracy of reports at various stages, you can determine the speed and see if the tolerance is getting better or worse. Basically, you can predict when machines need maintenance to keep them running within desirable specifications.

SMB IT Departments Five Years Out

How is all of this technology going to affect us five years from now? IT rooms and data centers will shrink in size as information moves to the cloud. Onsite will mostly include networking, lightweight storage, printing, and thin client desktop support. Services will be required to support this and the business processes, plus manage the service contracts with the providers and keep things running.

On the plus side, infrastructure will cost less, and the ability to expand or reduce users and licenses will be greatly simplified. This is a real benefit, as it allows the business to spend more time and effort on business issues instead of hardware, software, and infrastructure.

What's with Phone Systems?

Over time, phone systems will disappear. Products like Microsoft Lync could easily make them obsolete. The future belongs to unified communication systems and collaboration software. As phone systems age and require replacements, these new technologies will replace them.

What's with Email?

Tradition email servers will still be used for the electronic communication of documents. Historically, too much reliance has been placed on email for archiving of inter-business and departmental communication. However, this isn't the best place for this kind of information to be kept, because it's hidden from other parts of the business that may require it.

So, what is better than email? There are many different technologies that have been evolving for collaborating information within a company or across company boundaries. These applications are web-based document repositories that allow people to share information. Take a look at Slack, Jive, and Microsoft Lync to name a few. There are even some mail servers evolving that incorporate these technologies. Zafara is a popular replacement to Exchange, which now has some very interesting collaboration tools. Do some research and find out what works for your business.

Ultimately, stick with lightweight web-based tools, because they can more easily be layered and integrated into systems.

The Future of Management

Management must also change with technology as we move into the future. It's not reasonable or realistic to believe that one person can know it all. We all need to know our limits and work together to build the future.

The following quotes about management are definitely worth reading:

There are leaders and there are those who lead. Leaders hold a position of power or authority, but those who lead inspire us. Whether they're individuals or organizations, we follow those who lead, not because we have to, but because we want to. We follow those who lead, not for them, but for ourselves.

-

Simon Sinek

Leadership is not about the next election, it is about the next generation

-

Simon Sinek

If you want to be a great leader, remember to treat all people with respect at all times. For one because, you will never know when you will need their help. And two, it's a sign you respect people, which all great leaders do.

-

Simon Sinek

Panic causes tunnel vision. Calm acceptance of danger allows us to

more easily assess the situation and
see the options.

Simon Sinek

Future Trends Concluded

The information is this chapter covers some current trends in the industry. This technology isn't new or earth shattering, but it is very important for you to learn about it at some point in your career. Remember to find the trend and ride the wave. In your five-year plan, identify where things are going, and start putting the tools and technology that is useful for your business in place today. Adapt and change your five-year plan accordingly. Know your people, know the business you are in, follow the trends, and make use of the tools that are suitable.

Change is inevitable, so what makes sense today may not be right tomorrow. For example, UNIX was the standard for high-end engineering workstations for many years. UNIX tools and software was mature, fast, stable, and easy to manage. Then along came low-cost PCs that were slower (at first), flakey, and complex to manage. However, over time, they improved. Eventually, they became the new standard.

Moving forward, this will change again. VDI is here and will change the engineering desktop of the future.

Chapter 21

21 Closing

Throughout this book, I hope that you've found some useful tools and techniques that can be used to support a manufacturing-based SMB and position it for the future of IT technology.

Based on my background in manufacturing and experience with IT, I've provided examples of methods and techniques that have worked well for me. I hope that this leads you along the path to a prosperous future.

Here are some important points to remember:

• Use as many built-in tools as possible

• Discover the core foundation components of your business

• Don't upgrade all computers to the latest updates; set up a test group

• Plan everything before you do it

• Document everything, and save documents for easy retrieval

• Get organized

• Centrally manage as much as possible

- Know the business and how to adapt

- Learn how to address both operational IT and special projects to enhance the business

- Deliver applications securely

- Keep things simple

Come checkout my website at www.doitlean.ca, I will be adding to this site and be including some tools that you will find useful. Thank you and I hope you enjoyed the journey.

References

Guts the seven laws of business that make Chrysler the worlds hottest car company by *Robert A Lutz,* Published by John Wiley & Sons, 1998

How to implement Lean Manufacturing by *Lonnie Wilson,* McGraw Hill, 2010

The new rational Manager by *Charles H. Kepner and Benjamin B Tregor,,* Princeton Research Press, 2013

Do what you are by *Paul D. Tieger and Barbara Barron,* Little Brown and Company Hachette Book Group